Robert J. Dixson

New Edition

Book 3

MODERN AMERICAN ENGLISH

Prentice Hall Regents, Englewood Cliffs, NJ 07632

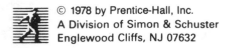
Printed in the United States of America

10 9 8 7 6 5

ISBN 0-13-543026-7

Prentice-Hall International (UK) Limited, *London*
Prentice-Hall of Australia Pty. Limited, *Sydney*
Prentice-Hall Canada Inc., *Toronto*
Prentice-Hall Hispanoamericana, S.A., *Mexico*
Prentice-Hall of India Private Limited, *New Delhi*
Prentice-Hall of Japan, Inc., *Tokyo*
Simon & Schuster Asia Pte. Ltd., *Singapore*
Editora Prentice-Hall do Brasil, Ltda., *Rio de Janeiro*

Table of Contents

Preface

Modern American English,Textbook Three, is the third of a series of six texts, with correlated workbooks and recordings, designed as a complete course of study in English as a second language. The first two books provide elementary vocabulary and lay the foundations for a comprehension of the principles of English grammar; taken together, they can be considered to comprise a beginning course in English. The remaining books, the workbooks, and the recordings build upon this foundation by expanding the study of vocabulary and completing the survey of English grammatical structures. Book Six, although primarily a reader, provides a general review and additional practice on all the material previously studied.

The six books of the series have been planned for use in the usual junior high school, high school, or adult course of study. The pace of the books, therefore, is measured but intensive, as is proper for students studying English on this level. Extensive oral practice is provided for eveything presented. Students are prepared to move, without difficulty or confusion, from one step to the next, from one lesson to the following lesson. Vocabulary and grammar are controlled at all times, particularly at the beginning and intermediate levels in Textbooks One through Four. Consequently, there is no danger of teaching more vocabulary or structure than a student can readily absorb.

Expressed in a different way, the purpose of this book, as well as of the remaining books of the series, is to teach students how to use and understand spoken English. The approach emphasizes at all times the ability of the students to use what they have studied. All materials and all activities in the series contribute directly to this end.

Modern American English, Textbook Three, is simple to use and easy to follow. It is a basic textbook, consisting of fifteen lessons. Every fifth lesson is a review that provides additional practice on the material that has been covered in the previous four lessons. Each of the remaining lessons is divided into four sections: *Reading and Oral Practice; Structure and Pattern Practice; Pronunciation and Intonation Practice;* and *General Practice.* Each of these sections is intended to give a particular kind of practice that will strengthen the students' learning experience and lead to their ability to communicate in the new language.

1. Reading and Oral Practice. This section introduces the material that is to be studied in the lesson. It usually consists of a series of questions and answers that are cued to pictures. This introductory material is usually connected into a brief narrative. Most of the lessons present both structural material—verb tenses, possessive forms, and so on—and cultural material—addresses, directions, articles of clothing, colors, and so on. In addition, there are short dialogues that introduce the students to the conversational uses of the structural patterns they have been studying.

The first part of each section is intended primarily for listening and repeating practice. That is, the students should listen while the teacher reads the sentences; then the students should repeat them after the teacher in chorus; third, individual students should be asked to repeat both questions and answers; and finally, individual students should read the sentences, both questions and answers.

In the next section, the students answer questions based on the previous material that are cued to the same or similar pictures. The teacher should first go over this section as a listening practice, giving both questions and answers; choral and individual repetition should follow; then the teacher should ask the questions while individual students give the answers. As a final step, one student asks the questions and another student gives the answers. This kind of student-student practice is highly recommended for all the exercises throughout the book.

Generally, the structural and cultural material is presented separately but in the same manner, that is, with a listen-repeat practice first and a question-and-answer practice second.

Similar procedures should be followed for the dialogues—listening, choral and individual repetition, teacher-student practice, and student-student practice.

2. Structure and Pattern Practice. This section is devoted to the study of the grammatical structures and idiomatic expressions in English. The section begins with a careful explanation of the structure that is being presented in the lesson. Notes are also included on the idiomatic and cultural material that has been included in the *Reading and Oral Practice*.

The explanatory note is followed by a wide variety of drills that give the students a command of the forms of the different patterns of English. It is suggested that the teacher first go through each exercise orally, with students repeating each cue and its answer in chorus. In the next step, the teacher should present the cue and then ask the class to give the answer in chorus. After that, the teacher should give the cue, with individual students giving the answer. There should be immediate correction of wrong answers, first by giving the right one and then having the students repeat it in chorus.

When sufficient oral work has been done, the teacher can assign the exercises as written homework. Homework should be corrected carefully and returned to the students so that they can note their errors and observe their progress. The exercises in this section are designed for habit formation on specific patterns, whereas the conversation practice in the final section of the lesson is designed to give the students greater flexibility in the *use* of the patterns.

3. Pronunciation and Intonation Practice. This section gives practice on different aspects of pronunciation. In this particular book, each lesson contains minimal pair drills on contrasted sounds. Many words are given in these drills that are NOT intended for vocabulary study, but ONLY for pronunciation practice. For intonation practice, special exercises are marked with intonation patterns.

The material in this section should be presented by means of repetition, both choral and individual. The teacher's pronunciation and intonation will serve as a model for the students. The sentences for intonation practice should be said at a natural conversational speed so that the students will become accustomed to the sound of English as it is actually spoken. The recordings give valuable additional practice for this section.

4. General Practice. This section gives oral practice in the actual use of English for conversational purposes. The exercise in this section is a question-and-answer practice based on the material that has been presented previously in the lesson.

The procedures for the practice in this section should consist first of teacher-student practice, and second of student-student practice. In the teacher-student practice, the teacher asks the questions or gives the commands, while individual students respond. In student-student practice, one student acts as teacher, while another makes the appropriate responses.

Additional practice is given in the Teacher's Manual in the form of conversation practice. There are questions the students can answer from their own experience and knowledge within the structural and cultural framework of the patterns and vocabulary that have been studied. These exercises are only suggestions. Each teacher should work out the particular exercise, with appropriate questions and commands, before giving it to the students, so that it will conform to the reality of that particular classroom and group of students.

Supplementary Material. A Teacher's Manual is available for each level of this series. There are also companion workbooks available for each textbook. Each workbook lesson is closely coordinated with the corresponding lesson in the appropriate textbook. The workbooks give additional material to help build all four of the language skills—listening, speaking, reading, and writing. In addition, there are recordings that cover the material in each of the textbook lessons, thereby giving the students a valuable source for more oral practice.

Lesson 1

1. Reading and Oral Practice

A. Listen and repeat.

What does Dick want to do?
He wants to buy a new car.

How long has he had his car?
He's had the same car for three years.

What's wrong with it?
It's worn out and needs a lot of
    repairs.

Was it a new or used car?
It was a used car.

What has he decided?
He's decided not to buy another used
    car.

Has he been to any used car dealers?
No, he's been to several new car dealers.

Have they offered him a good price for his old car?
They haven't offered him a good enough price for his old car.

Why hasn't he bought a car yet?
Because he hasn't found a real bargain yet.

What's he going to do?
He's going to keep on looking for a while.

B. Answer the questions.

1. What does Dick want to do?

2. How long has he had his car?

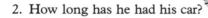

3. What's wrong with it?

4. Was it a new or used car?

5. What has he decided?

6. Has he been to any used car dealers?

7. Have they offered him a good price for his old car?

8. Why hasn't he bought a car yet?

9. What's he going to do?

C. Listen and repeat.

What do pints, quarts, and gallons measure?
They measure liquids.

What's an example of a liquid?
Milk is a liquid.

What are some other liquids?
Water and orange juice are also liquids.

Which is the smallest, a pint, a quart, or a gallon?
A pint is the smallest.
Which is the largest, a pint, a quart, or a gallon?
A gallon is the largest.

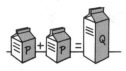

How many pints are there in a quart?
There are two pints in a quart.

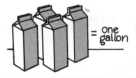

How many quarts are there in a gallon?
There are four quarts in a gallon.

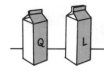

How does a quart compare with a liter?
They're almost the same size, but a liter is a little larger.

D. Answer the questions.

1. What do pints, quarts, and gallons measure?

2. What's an example of a liquid?

3. What are some other liquids?

4. Which is the smallest, a pint, a quart, or a gallon?

   Which is the largest, a pint, a quart, or a gallon?

5. How many pints are there in a quart?

6. How many quarts are there in a gallon?

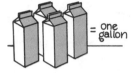

7. How does a quart compare with a liter?

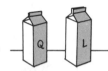

E. Dialogue.

LINDA: Where have you been?
DICK: I've been at the garage since four o'clock.
LINDA: What happened?
DICK: My car broke down again.
LINDA: Have you gotten it back yet?
DICK: No, they haven't finished with it yet.
LINDA: When will you get it?
DICK: I won't get it until Friday.
LINDA: Well, at least you'll have it in time for the weekend.
DICK: But I won't have any money, and I'm going out on a date with Cathy. The repairs are going to cost a lot.
LINDA: Have you looked for a new car?
DICK: Yes, I've looked and looked.
LINDA: Have you found a good one?
DICK: No, I haven't found a real bargain yet.

2. Structure and Pattern Practice

The present perfect is formed with the auxiliary verb *to have* and the past participle of the main verb.

I have (I've) moved	we have (we've) moved
you have (you've) moved	you have (you've) moved
he has (he's) moved	
she has (she's) moved	they have (they've) moved
it has (it's) moved	

The contracted forms in parentheses are generally used in conversation.

The past participle is the third principal part of English verbs. With regular verbs, it is the same as the past tense form; that is, it is formed by adding -d or -ed to the simple form of the verb.

to move	moved	moved
to start	started	started
to study	studied	studied

Irregular verbs have irregular past participles as well as past tense forms. These forms for the irregular verbs used in Books One, Two, and Three can be found in the Appendix on p. 143.

Questions are formed by placing the auxiliary before the subject. Negatives are formed by placing *not* after the auxiliary. The contracted forms *haven't* and *hasn't* are generally used in conversation and informal writing.

Has your car broken down again?
They haven't returned my car yet.

One use of the present perfect tense is to describe an action that took place at some indefinite time in the past.

I've seen that movie.
We've read that book.

The action can be a single or a repeated action.

I've only talked to him once.
I've talked to her several times.

The present perfect is also used for an action that began in the past and continues up to the present time.

He's studied accounting for six months.
They've lived in the same house since 1974.

7

For in this use shows the length of time the action has continued. *Since* indicates the point in time when the action began.

Note that *enough* follows the adjective that it modifies.

> He can't find a good enough bargain.
> I don't have a warm enough coat.

One can be used as a pronoun to avoid the repetition of a noun. The plural form *ones* is also used in the same way.

> He wants to buy a new car, but he can't get a good price for his old one.
> She needed a coat, but the ones in the store were too expensive.

The following irregular verbs are used in this lesson:

to buy	bought	bought
to break	broke	broken
to cost	cost	cost
to keep (on)	kept	kept

Exercises

A. Change these sentences to the present perfect. Omit the time expression from the present perfect sentences.

E X A M P L E
I saw my adviser yesterday. *I've seen my adviser.*

1. He left for the airport at four o'clock.
2. He spent a lot of money last night.
3. We began a new lesson last week.
4. His car broke down last night.

B. Change to questions.

E X A M P L E
I've seen my adviser. (you) *Have you seen your adviser?*

1. We've paid our tuition. (you)
2. It's rained a lot this spring.
3. He's been in Chicago this week.
4. They've copied the new words in their notebooks.

C. Change to the negative.

E X A M P L E

I've seen my adviser. *I haven't seen my adviser.*

1. She's looked at her schedule.
2. My adviser has approved my schedule.
3. They've registered for the semester.
4. He's taught physics.

D. Complete these sentences with *for* or *since* and the phrase in parentheses.

E X A M P L E

I haven't seen my adviser. (two months) *I haven't seen my adviser for two months.*

1. He's worked at the gasoline station. (one month)
2. I haven't seen my adviser. (October)
3. They've been at lunch. (noon)
4. He's been at the post office. (two hours)
5. They've lived in the city. (1972)
6. She's worked for the same company. (three years)

E. Substitute *one* or *ones* for the *italicized* noun in each of these sentences.

E X A M P L E

He has an old car, but he wants to get a new *car*. *He has an old car, but he wants to get a new one.*

1. He must get new tires because his old *tires* have worn out.
2. My new coat is warmer than my old *coat*.
3. This bus goes to the mountains, but that *bus* goes to the beach.
4. The old office was crowded, but the new *office* has a lot of space.

3. Pronunciation and Intonation Practice

A. Listen and repeat.

EXAMPLE

(Teacher)   When will you get it back?

(Students)   When will you get it back?

(Teacher)   When will you get it back?

---

1. When will I find a real bargain?
2. When will he finish the inventory?
3. When will you see your adviser?
4. When will we have the exam?
5. When will he leave for Chicago?

B. Repeat several times.

[o] as the *oa* in *coat*	[e] as the *a* in *ate*
oat	ate
boat	bait
goat	gate
load	laid
mode	made
Joan	Jane
comb	came
foam	fame
cope	cape
soak	sake
groan	grain

4. General Practice

Answer the questions.

1. What time did school begin today?
2. How long have you been at school today?
3. What time did your English class begin today?
4. How long have you been in your English class today?
5. How many pages have you finished in this book?
6. How many days a week do you have English?
7. How many days have you had English this week?

Lesson 2

1. Reading and Oral Practice
A. Listen and repeat.

Who's Laura West?
She's Steve West's wife.

Why did she have lunch with him
   yesterday?
She'd come to town to go shopping.

Did she find any bargains at the
   stores?
She found a lot of bargains. There are
   always a lot of sales in January.

What did she buy?
She bought some shirts for her
   husband.

Did she get a good bargain?
Yes, they'd cut the price on shirts
   forty percent.

Why didn't Steve buy his own shirts?
He'd looked, but he hadn't found any
inexpensive ones.

What else did Laura look at?
After she'd had lunch, she looked at
furniture.

Did she buy anything else?
She bought some sheets after she'd
been to several stores.

B. Answer the questions.

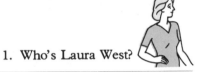

1. Who's Laura West?

2. Why did she have lunch with him
yesterday?

3. Did she find any bargains at the
stores?

4. What did she buy?

5. Did she get a good bargain?

6. Why didn't Steve buy his own shirts?

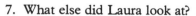

7. What else did Laura look at?

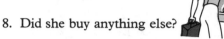

8. Did she buy anything else?

C. Listen and repeat.

How was the weather yesterday?
It was very hot.
What was the temperature?
It was ninety degrees.

How cold is the temperature in the winter?
It gets as low as ten degrees in the winter.
Is that centigrade?
No, that's Fahrenheit.

What's the freezing point of water on the centigrade scale?
It's zero degrees.
What's the freezing point on the Fahrenheit scale?
It's thirty-two degrees.

What happens to water when it
freezes?
When water freezes, it changes to ice.

D. Answer the questions.

1. How was the weather yesterday?

   What was the temperature?

2. How cold is the temperature in the
   winter?

   Is that centigrade?

3. What's the freezing point of water
   on the centigrade scale?

   What's the freezing point on the
   Fahrenheit scale?

4. What happens to water when it
   freezes?

E. Dialogue.

SALLY: I didn't see Dick last night.
TOM: He didn't come to school.
SALLY: What was the matter?
TOM: He said that he'd had an accident.
SALLY: Oh, that's too bad! I hope that he's all right.
TOM: He's okay, but he said that he'd really smashed up the car.
SALLY: How did it happen?
TOM: The street was wet, and he skidded into a telephone pole.
SALLY: That car was no good. Does he have insurance?
TOM: He said that he'd just taken out new insurance.
SALLY: I hope that he'll get enough money for a new car.
TOM: He said that he'd spoken to the insurance agent right away.
SALLY: And how much will he get?
TOM: Well, he's out looking for a new car right now.

2. Structure and Pattern Practice

The past perfect is most frequently used for an action that took place before some definite point in the past; that is, it is the past tense of the simple past. It most often occurs in connection with some past time, either stated or implied.

> He said that he'd had an accident. (He made the statement in the past, and the accident happened before the statement.)

> After she'd had lunch, she bought some sheets. (First she had lunch and then she bought the sheets. Both actions were in the past, but the lunch took place first.)

The past perfect is formed with the auxiliary *had* and the past participle of the main verb.

I had (I'd) begun	we had (we'd) begun
you had (you'd) begun	you had (you'd) begun
he had (he'd) begun	
she had (she'd) begun	they had (they'd) begun
it had begun	

The contracted forms given in parentheses are generally used in conversation.

Questions are formed by placing the auxiliary before the subject. Negatives are formed by placing *not* after the auxiliary. The contracted form *hadn't* is generally used in conversation and informal writing.

> Had he taken out new insurance?
> He hadn't spoken to his insurance agent yet.

Own is used after possessive forms and strengthens the idea of possession.

> He always packs his own bag.
> Ann and Dick have their own friends.

The following irregular verbs are used for the first time in this lesson:

to cut	cut	cut
to freeze	froze	frozen
to speak	spoke	spoken

The plural of *wife* is *wives*.

Exercises

A. Change these sentences so that they begin with *He said that*. Change the past tense to the past perfect.

E X A M P L E
He saw his adviser. *He said that he'd seen his adviser.*

1. She laughed at his jokes.
2. They cut the prices on shirts by forty percent.
3. He spoke to the teacher about his schedule.
4. He was at the garage.
5. The water froze during the night.
6. He forgot all about his homework.

B. Change to questions.

E X A M P L E
He'd missed his class that evening. *Had he missed his class that evening?*

1. She'd learned to speak English in school.
2. He'd ordered the supplies.
3. I'd finished the inventory. (you)
4. They'd attended several meetings.
5. She'd gotten very good grades.

C. Change to the negative.

E X A M P L E
He'd caught the five o'clock plane. *He hadn't caught the five o'clock plane.*

1. They'd gone skiing over the weekend.
2. She'd bought some sheets.
3. He'd flown to San Francisco.
4. I'd looked at the schedule.
5. We'd paid our tuition.

D. Combine these sentences so that the first one becomes a time clause with *after* and a past perfect verb form.

She went to several stores. She bought some sheets. *After she'd gone to several stores, she bought some sheets.*

1. She went shopping. She went home with her husband.
2. He had lunch with his wife. He returned to the office.
3. He had an accident. He spoke to his insurance agent.
4. He checked the oil. He cleaned the windshield.
5. She spoke to her adviser. She paid her tuition.
6. He saw Ann. He went to the cafeteria.

E. Combine these sentences so that the first one uses a past perfect verb form and the second becomes a time clause with *before*.

She went to several stores. She met her husband. *She'd gone to several stores before she met her husband.*

1. She stood in line for an hour. She registered for her courses.
2. He took out new insurance. He had the accident.
3. She spoke to her adviser. She registered for her courses.
4. He attended several meetings. He went to his hotel.
5. He studied programming. He got his new job.
6. He finished the inventory. He ordered the office supplies.

3. Pronunciation and Intonation Practice

A. Repeat several times.

One syllable	*Two syllables*	
won't	shouldn't	haven't
can't	mustn't	hasn't
		hadn't

B. Listen and repeat.

E X A M P L E

(Teacher)   He has his own room.

(Students) He has his own room.

(Teacher)   He has his own room.

---

1. He bought his own car.
2. He packs his own bag.
3. I do my own work.
4. I need my own notebook.
5. She has her own pencil.

C. Repeat several times.

[o] as the *oa* in *coat*   [ɔ] as the *au* in *caught*

Joe	jaw
low	law
coat	caught
boat	bought
bowl	ball
cold	called

4. General Practice

Perform the actions and answer the questions.

1. Write the word *centigrade*.
   What did you do? (I)
2. Write the word *Fahrenheit*.
   What did you do?
3. What had you done before you wrote *Fahrenheit*?
4. What lesson are you studying now?
5. What lesson had you studied before you began Lesson 2?

Lesson 3

1. Reading and Oral Practice

A. Listen and repeat.

Whose birthday was it yesterday?
It was Dick's birthday.

How old was he?
He was twenty-four years old.

Did his family give him any presents?
His parents gave him a wristwatch.
    His sister gave him a tape recorder.

Who sent him birthday cards?
His aunt and uncle sent him birthday
    cards.

What did his friends do?
They took him out for dinner.

What did his friends bring him?
They brought him a compass for his new car.

Who gave Dick the best present of all?
Dick's boss gave him the best present of all.

What did he give him?
He gave him a better job. He'll be a programmer in the accounting department.

B. Answer the questions.

1. Whose birthday was it yesterday?

2. How old was he?

3. Did his family give him any presents?

4. Who sent him birthday cards?

5. What did his friends do?

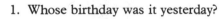

21

6. What did his friends bring him?

7. Who gave Dick the best present of all?

8. What did he give him?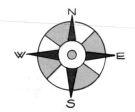

C. Listen and repeat.

What does a compass show?
It shows directions.
What are the four points of the compass?
They are north, south, east, and west.

What's east of the United States?
The Atlantic Ocean is east of the
  United States.

What's west of the United States?
The Pacific Ocean is west of the
  United States.

Is New York on the East Coast or the
  West Coast?
It's on the East Coast.

Is San Francisco on the East Coast or the West Coast?
It's on the West Coast.

What country is north of the United States?
Canada is north of the United States.

What country is south of the United States?
Mexico is south of the United States.

D. Answer the questions.

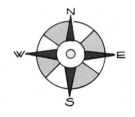

1. What does a compass show?
2. What are the four points of the compass?

3. What's east of the United States?

4. What's west of the United States?

5. Is New York on the East Coast or the West Coast?

6. Is San Francisco on the East Coast or the West Coast?

7. What country is north of the United States?

8. What country is south of the United States?

E. Dialogue.

SALLY: Where are you going?

MIKE: I'm going downtown. I'm in a hurry.

SALLY: I can see that. What's the matter?

MIKE: I need to rent a typewriter.

SALLY: What happened to yours?

MIKE: Mine is in the repair shop. It broke down last week.

SALLY: Can't you borrow one?

MIKE: Bill's using his this weekend. He and I have the same problem.

SALLY: And what's the problem?

MIKE: We have to finish a term paper for our sociology class.

SALLY: What about Linda? She must have a typewriter.

MIKE: She has one, but she left hers at home.

SALLY: Well, I have one too. I can lend you mine.

MIKE: Oh, thank you! That's really nice of you.

2. Structure and Pattern Practice

A few verbs like *to give* are followed by two objects, a direct and an indirect object. The indirect object follows the verb, and the direct object comes after it.

> He lent me his typewriter.
> I wrote her a letter.
> They gave him a better job.
> We bought them a gift.

Note that the indirect object is usually a person (or an institution) and the direct object is usually a thing.

An alternate form is a prepositional phrase beginning with *to* (or *for* in a few cases) which comes after the direct object.

> He lent his typewriter to me.
> I wrote a letter to her.
> They gave a better job to him.
> We bought a gift for them.

In American usage, when both the indirect and direct objects are pronouns, the prepositional phrase form is always used.

> He lent it to me.
> We gave it to them.

In addition to the possessive adjectives, there are also possessive pronoun forms.

I	my	mine
you	your	yours
he	his	his
she	her	hers
it	its	
we	our	ours
they	their	theirs

> My typewriter is in the repair shop. Can you lend me yours?
> My schedule is very easy, but hers is heavy.

Note that there is no possessive pronoun form for *it*. Also note that an apostrophe (') is NOT used with these forms.

Aunts are the sisters of one's father or mother. *Uncles* are the brothers of one's father or mother. *Cousins* are the children of one's aunts and uncles. A *cousin* can be male or female.

In English, one borrows something *from* someone, and lends something *to* someone.

> I need to borrow a typewriter from someone.
> Can you lend yours to me?

Irregular verbs introduced in this lesson are:

to bring	brought	brought
to lend	lent	lent
to show	showed	shown

Exercises

A. Change these sentences so that they use an indirect object in place of the prepositional phrase.

E X A M P L E

I sent a postcard to my cousin. *I sent my cousin a postcard.*

1. He showed the report to me.
2. They gave a wristwatch to Dick for his birthday.
3. I'll write a letter to you next week.
4. She made some coffee for her boss.
5. She brings the mail to her boss in the morning.
6. His sister got a tape recorder for him.

B. Change these sentences so that they use a prepositional phrase in place of the indirect object.

E X A M P L E

I sent my cousin a postcard. (to) *I sent a postcard to my cousin.*

1. He wrote his uncle a letter. (to)
2. He got the boss some stamps. (for)

3. She gave the students an exam. (to)
4. He taught them the new lesson. (to)
5. I read her the letter. (to)
6. She bought him some tapes. (for)

C. Change the direct and indirect objects to object pronouns and then rearrange the sentences in the correct order.

E X A M P L E
She sent her uncle the postcard. *She sent it to him.*

1. They're going to lend Dick a radio.
2. He showed Tom and me the tape recorder.
3. They showed their friends their new house.
4. He sent Ann the package.

D. Add the expression in parentheses to these sentences.

E X A M P L E
I sent a birthday card. (my cousin) *I sent my cousin a birthday card.*

1. She taught the new words last week. (us)
2. She read the new sentences. (to the students)
3. I'm going to lend it. (to you)
4. I showed my presents. (to my cousin)

E. Change the italicized words to the appropriate possessive pronoun.

E X A M P L E
I need to borrow your typewriter because *my typewriter* broke down.
  I need to borrow your typewriter because mine broke down.

1. We rode downtown in their car. *Our car* was in the garage.
2. My boss is very tall. *Her boss* is very short.
3. Our school is a large one. *Their school* is small.
4. She spoke to her teacher, but I didn't speak to *my teacher.*
5. I gave the teacher my notebook, but you didn't give her *your notebook.*
6. I found my pencil, but I didn't find *his pencil.*

27

3. Pronunciation and Intonation Practice

A. Listen and repeat.

E X A M P L E

(Teacher)   We gave it to them.

(Students)   We gave it to them.

(Teacher)   We gave it to them.

---

1. I sent it to her.
2. They showed it to me.
3. He read it to us.

4. She got them for me.
5. He taught it to me.

B. Repeat several times.

[a] as the *o* in *not*	[ɔ] as the *au* in *caught*
not	naught
tot	taught
cot	caught
Don	dawn
collar	caller

4. General Practice

Perform the actions and then answer the questions.

1. Please give your book, pencil, or something else to a student in your class.
2. What did you give the student?
3. Who did you give it to?
4. Please show another student your book, pencil, or something else.
5. What did you show the student?
6. Who did you show it to?

Lesson 4

1. Reading and Oral Practice

A. Listen and repeat.

What kind of restaurant is a cafeteria?
A cafeteria is a self-service restaurant.

Is there a cafeteria at the college?
Yes, there's a big one. The students
  can help themselves to both hot and
  cold food.

How are the prices?
The prices are very low.

Is it popular with the students?
Yes, it's very popular with the
  students.

When do they go to the cafeteria?
They go to the cafeteria for lunch.
  They also go there after classes.

29

What do they do there after classes?
They meet each other and sit and
    talk.

What's Mike doing now?
He's getting himself a hamburger.

What's Linda doing?
She's sitting by herself and reading a
    book.

B. Answer the questions.

1. What kind of restaurant is a
   cafeteria?

2. Is there a cafeteria at the college?

3. How are the prices?

4. Is it popular with the students?

5. When do they go to the cafeteria?

6. What do they do there after classes?

7. What's Mike doing now?

8. What's Linda doing?

C. Listen and repeat.

What's his address?
It's 24 East Summer Street.

Where's their apartment?
It's at 2386 South School Street.

Where does he live?
He lives at 922 East 11th Street.

Where does he work?
He works in a building on South Main Street.

Where does she live?
She lives at 1748 West 96th Street.

31

Where does she work?
She works on Seventh Avenue.

D. Answer the questions.

1. What's his address?

3. Where does he live?

4. Where does he work?

6. Where does she work?

E. Dialogue.

SUSAN: What do you have there?
MIKE: I bought myself some new records.
SUSAN: Do you want to hear them now?
MIKE: I thought that your record player was out of order.
SUSAN: It was, but I fixed it.
MIKE: Who helped you?
SUSAN: Nobody helped me. I fixed it all by myself.
MIKE: That's good. I didn't know that you could do things like that yourself.
SUSAN: Let's go and try it out.
MIKE: Okay. Let's ask Linda. She's sitting over there by herself.
SUSAN: She's studying. We should study for the math exam ourselves.
MIKE: Okay, but let's listen to my records first.

2. Structure and Pattern Practice

Reflexive pronouns in English have the ending *self* in the singular and *selves* in the plural.

myself	ourselves
yourself	yourselves
himself	
herself	themselves
itself	

Note that there are different forms for the singular and plural of *you*.

Reflexive pronouns generally refer back to the subject.

> The little girl dresses herself every morning.
> He cut himself yesterday morning.

They are also used as intensive pronouns to give emphasis to a person or thing.

> The boss himself will talk to the salesman.

They are also used with the preposition *by* to express the idea of *alone*, or *without help*.

> She's sitting over there by herself.
> I did the homework by myself.

When an address is given that includes both street and number, the preposition *at* is used. When only the street is given, it is introduced by the preposition *on*.

> She lives at 1748 West 96th Street.
> She works on Seventh Avenue.

When the number of an address has more than two digits, the number is said in two parts, as in the examples below.

> He lives at 922 (nine twenty-two) East 11th Street.
> Their apartment is at 2386 (twenty-three eighty-six) South
>   School Street.

Let's, a contracted form for *let us*, is used to introduce an imperative sentence that includes the speaker. The contracted form is almost always used both in conversation and writing. The negative is *let's not*.

> Let's listen to your records now.
> Let's not study for a while.

To sit is an irregular verb.

> to sit   sat   sat

Exercises

A. Complete these sentences with the correct reflexive pronoun.

E X A M P L E

Jim bought __*himself*__ some records.

1. We got _____ some hot food.
2. Mike likes to talk about _____.
3. Susan also likes to talk about _____.
4. The men like to talk about _____.
5. Do you like to talk about _____?
6. I don't like to talk about _____.

B. Add the appropriate intensive pronouns to these sentences. First place the pronoun directly after the subject. Then place it at the end of the sentence.

E X A M P L E

Mr. West talked to the salesman. *Mr. West himself talked to the salesman. Mr. West talked to the salesman himself.*

1. We took the packages to the post office.
2. Dick fixed his record player.
3. Miss Black wrote that letter.
4. You must clean your dormitory rooms.
5. The typists write all the letters.
6. Mike, you must talk to the teacher.

C. Substitute *by* and the appropriate intensive pronoun for *alone* or *without help* in these sentences.

E X A M P L E

Linda is sitting over there alone. *Linda is sitting over there by herself.*

1. I like to listen to my records alone.
2. The girls cleaned the house without help.
3. He took a vacation alone.
4. Mike and Jim like to study alone.
5. Did you try to change the tire without help?
6. You boys shouldn't sit over there alone.

D. Change these sentences to the imperative with *let's*. **If the sentence is negative, use** *let's not.*

We listened to the new records. *Let's listen to the new records.*

---

1. We ate in the cafeteria.
2. We didn't attend the sociology lecture.
3. We sat near the blackboard.
4. We tried to fix the record player ourselves.
5. We didn't clean the house this weekend.
6. We studied for the exam.

3. Pronunciation and Intonation Practice

A. Listen and repeat.

(Teacher)   It will be good for her.

(Students)   It will be good for her.

(Teacher)   It will be good for her.

---

1. It's easy for us.
2. It's very hard for them.
3. That will be bad for you.
4. I've read enough of it.
5. I was very happy about it.

B. Repeat several times.

[ɔ] as the *aw* in *saw*   [aʊ] as the *ow* in *now*

gnaw	now
saw	sow
clawed	cloud
dawn	down
gone	gown
fall	foul
all	owl

4. General Practice

Use the addresses given to answer the question *Where do they live?*

E X A M P L E

Where do they live? (1025 First Avenue) *They live at 1025 First Avenue.*

---

1. 1967 East School Street
2. West Spring Street
3. 2328 North Main Street
4. 178 South Summer Street
5. 1384 East 85th Street
6. Tenth Avenue
7. New York Avenue
8. 1818 East Winter Street
9. Main Street
10. 1281 South First Avenue

Lesson 5

REVIEW

1. Review of Structure and Pattern Practice

A. Change to the present perfect. Omit the time expression from the present perfect sentence.

E X A M P L E

I saw my adviser yesterday. *I've seen my adviser.*

1. His car broke down last Tuesday.
2. He met the salesmen last week.
3. We heard the records last night.
4. I showed him the letter yesterday.
5. He lent me his typewriter last week.
6. He gave the teacher his term paper yesterday.

B. Change these sentences so that they begin with *He said that*. Change the past tense to the past perfect.

E X A M P L E

He saw his adviser. *He said that he'd seen his adviser.*

1. He slept late on Sunday morning.
2. He fixed his record player himself.
3. She bought some shirts for him.
4. He found some real bargains in the stores.
5. He rode to work on the bus.
6. They sent me a package.

C. Change to questions.

I've seen my adviser. (you) *Have you seen your adviser?*

1. They'd flown to Chicago.
2. It's rained a lot this spring.
3. The bus had stopped at the corner.
4. He'd discovered the coast of Brazil.
5. We've made a lot of trips this year. (you)
6. They've gone to the mountains to ski.

D. Change to the negative.

I've seen my adviser. *I haven't seen my adviser.*

1. We've had a heavy schedule this year.
2. It's snowed this year.
3. He'd attended the meeting.
4. He's been in class all day.
5. She's packed his bag for him.
6. He'd tried to fix the record player himself.

E. Complete these sentences with *for* or *since* and the phrase in parentheses.

I haven't seen my adviser. (two months). *I haven't seen my adviser for two months.*

1. He hadn't visited Chicago. (several years)
2. He hadn't visited Chicago. (1975)
3. It hasn't rained. (Monday)
4. I haven't heard any music. (a long time)
5. I haven't eaten in the cafeteria. (June)
6. They've been in the cafeteria. (more than an hour)

F. Combine these sentences using *after* and a past perfect verb form.

We studied the lesson. The teacher gave us an exam. *After we'd studied the lesson, the teacher gave us an exam.*

1. I drove to the city. I didn't find a place to park.
2. He went to night school. He got a better job.
3. She graduated from college. She taught chemistry.
4. He got a better job. He bought a new car.
5. It snowed. We went skiing.
6. He arrived in Chicago. He went to a hotel.

G. Change these sentences so that they use an indirect object in place of the prepositional phrase.

E X A M P L E

I sent a postcard to my cousin.   *I sent my cousin a postcard.*

---

1. They offered a new job to Steve West.
2. She gave extra homework to the good students.
3. She read the letter to her boss.
4. I showed my schedule to my adviser.

H. Change these sentences so that they use a prepositional phrase in place of the indirect object.

E X A M P L E

I sent my cousin a postcard. (to)   *I sent a postcard to my cousin.*

---

1. We showed the salesmen the computer. (to)
2. She read the students the new sentences. (to)
3. I bought my aunt a book. (for)
4. She got him some envelopes. (for)

I. Change the *italicized* words to the appropriate possessive pronoun.

E X A M P L E

I need to borrow your typewriter because *my typewriter* broke down.
   I need to borrow your typewriter because mine broke down.

---

1. I can't find my pen, but I found *your pen.*
2. I lent him my car because *his car* was in the garage.
3. I cleaned my room, but she didn't clean *her room.*
4. The teacher looked at your books, but she didn't look at *our books.*
5. I've seen your house, but I haven't seen *their house.*
6. I like your wristwatch, but I don't like *my wristwatch.*

J. Complete the sentences with the correct reflexive pronouns.

EXAMPLE

Ted bought __himself__ some records.

1. We found some expensive new coats for _____.
2. I've never hurt _____.
3. She knows _____ very well.
4. He likes _____ too much.
5. Do you always get _____ a birthday present?
6. Why do they talk about _____ all the time?

K. Substitute *by* and the appropriate intensive pronoun for *alone* or *without help* in these sentences.

EXAMPLE

Ann is sitting over there alone. *Ann is sitting over there by herself.*

1. My brother learned to read without help.
2. Did you learn to read English without help?
3. His desk is all alone in the corner.
4. I want to be alone today.
5. We eat dinner alone.
6. You must write the letters without help.

2. General Practice

A. Answer the questions.

1. What do quarts, gallons, and pints measure?

2. What's an example of a liquid?

3. Which is the smallest, a pint, a quart, or a gallon?

4. Which is the largest, a pint, a quart, or a gallon?

5. How many pints are there in a quart?

6. How many quarts are there in a gallon?

7. How does a quart compare with a liter?

8. What scale do Americans use to measure the temperature?

9. What's the freezing point of water on the Fahrenheit scale?

10. What's the freezing point of water on the centigrade scale?

B. Answer the questions.

1. What does a compass show?

2. What are the four points of the compass?

3. What's east of your country?

4. What's west of your country?

5. What's north of your country?

6. What's south of your country?

C. Use the addresses given to answer the question *Where do they live?*

EXAMPLE

Where do they live? (1716 Third Avenue) *They live at 1716 Third Avenue.*

---

1. Spring Street
2. 211 West 27th Street
3. 419 East 104th Street
4. 7234 North Eighth Avenue
5. 681 South Summer Street
6. School Street

Lesson 6

1. Reading and Oral Practice

A. Listen and repeat.

What was Linda doing last night?
She was taking care of the Wests'
children last night.

Where were Steve and Laura West?
They'd gone to a concert.

How old are the Wests' children?
They have a son who is seven years
old and a daughter who is four.

What did the children do at eight
o'clock?
They went to bed.

What did Linda do after they'd fallen
asleep?
After they'd fallen asleep, Linda began
to study in the living room.

What happened while she was studying?
The telephone rang.

Who was calling?
The Wests were calling.

What did they want?
They wanted to make sure that the children were all right.

Do they worry about the children?
Yes, they always worry about the children.

What did Linda do after she'd talked to the Wests?
After she'd talked to the Wests, Linda began to study again.

B. Answer the questions.

1. What was Linda doing last night?

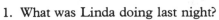

2. Where were Steve and Laura West?

3. How old are the Wests' children?

4. What did the children do at eight o'clock?

5. What did Linda do after they'd fallen asleep?

6. What happened while she was studying?

7. Who was calling?

8. What did they want?

9. Do they worry about the children?

10. What did Linda do after she'd talked to the Wests?

C. Listen and repeat.

Why was she carrying an umbrella?
She always carries an umbrella on cloudy days.

Why was he wearing a raincoat?
He always wears a raincoat on cloudy days.

Why was he wearing a jacket?
He always wears a jacket in the office.

Why was he wearing a necktie?
He always wears a tie in the office.

Why were they wearing their heavy overcoats?
They always wear their heavy overcoats on cold days.

Why was she wearing a good dress?
She always wears a good dress when she goes out.

Why was she wearing a skirt and blouse?
She always wears a skirt and blouse in the office.

Why were they wearing sweaters?
They always wear sweaters when it's windy and chilly.

D. Answer the questions.

1. Why was she carrying an umbrella?

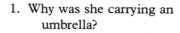

2. Why was he wearing a raincoat?

3. Why was he wearing a jacket?

4. Why was he wearing a necktie?

5. Why were they wearing their heavy overcoats?

6. Why was she wearing a good dress?

7. Why was she wearing a skirt and blouse?

8. Why were they wearing sweaters?

E. Dialogue.

RON: Why are you so happy?

SAM: Because the sun was shining when I got up this morning.

RON: Is that all?

SAM: And because I drove Linda to school this morning.

RON: Where did you meet her?

SAM: She was standing on the corner. She was waiting for her bus.

RON: Was she glad to see you?

SAM: Very glad. It was chilly and windy on that corner and she was only wearing slacks and a light blouse.

RON: What did you talk about?

SAM: Nothing serious. We joked and laughed.

2. Structure and Pattern Practice

The past continuous describes an action that was going on when another action in the past occurred.

The past continuous is not usually used alone. It is generally used in connection with another past time, either stated or implied.

> I was speaking to John when you arrived.
> It was raining when I left home.

Two actions that were taking place at the same time may both use the past continuous. They are often connected by *while*.

> I was studying my chemistry textbook while you were watching television.

The past continuous is formed with the past forms of *to be* and the present participle (the *-ing* form) of the main verb.

I was beginning	we were beginning
you were beginning	you were beginning
he was beginning	
she was beginning	they were beginning
it was beginning	

Questions are formed by placing the auxiliary before the subject. Negatives are formed by placing *not* after the auxiliary.

> Was she wearing a heavy coat?
> They weren't wearing their sweaters.

Child is an irregular noun. The plural form is *children*. A child can be either a girl or a boy.

The Wests refers to Mr. and Mrs. West, or to the entire West family.

Plural nouns form the possessive by adding an apostrophe (') after the plural ending.

> the boys' books
> the Wests' house
>
> the girls' pencils
> the Smiths' car

Irregular plural nouns—those not ending in *s*—form the possessive in the same way as singular nouns, by adding *'s*.

> the men's hats
> the women's coats

the children's room
the people's cars

Irregular verbs introduced in this lesson are:

to fall	fell	fallen
to ring	rang	rung
to shine	shone	shone

Exercises

A. Change these sentences to the past continuous. If the original sentence is a question or a negative, change it to the same form.

E X A M P L E

Did he wear a tie yesterday?   *Was he wearing a tie yesterday?*

---

1. I didn't look for the packages.
2. They began a new lesson yesterday morning.
3. She took care of the children last night.
4. The sun didn't shine yesterday.
5. I didn't look for shirts at the stores.
6. Did you fix your record player?

B. Combine these sentences, using *when* to connect them. The first sentence should be changed to the past continuous.

E X A M P L E

I drove to school. I saw her on the corner.   *I was driving to school when I saw her on the corner.*

---

1. He drove to work. The car broke down.
2. She attended a lecture. She met her friends.
3. You talked to Mr. West. His telephone rang.
4. I wrote my term paper. My typewriter broke down.
5. We walked to school. It began to rain.
6. He got himself a hamburger. I saw him.

C. Combine these sentences, using *while* to connect them. Both sentences should be changed to the past continuous.

E X A M P L E

She smiled. I talked to her. *She was smiling while I was talking to her.*

1. I studied. I ate.
2. I tried to read. She talked on the telephone.
3. It rained. We drove to work.
4. The children slept. I watched television.
5. Mrs. West cleaned the house. Mr. West slept.
6. He taught physics. I attended that school.

D. Complete these sentences with the possessive form of the noun in parentheses.

E X A M P L E

The ___*boys'*___ (boys) books are on their desks.

1. The _____ (Smiths) car is in the garage today.
2. They moved the _____ (typists) desks to a large office.
3. I found the _____ (children) hats in the living room.
4. His _____ (parents) house is a long way from here.
5. He reads all the _____ (salesmen) letters.
6. The _____ (girls) coats are in the living room.

3. Pronunciation and Intonation Practice

A. Listen and repeat.

E X A M P L E

(Teacher)   They always worry about the children.

(Students)   They always worry about the children.

(Teacher)   They always worry about the children.

1. We never talk about school.
2. He always gets to work early.

3. She never gets good grades.
4. It always rains in the spring.
5. He always checks the oil.

B. Repeat several times.

[au] as the *ow* in *now*   [u] as the *oo* in *school*

now	new
how	who
crowd	crude
foul	fool
noun	noon
town	tune
shout	shoot

4. General Practice.

Answer the questions.

E X A M P L E

What's he wearing?   *He's wearing a hat.*   hat

1. What are they wearing?   sweaters

2. What's she wearing?   skirt and blouse

3. What's he wearing?   a shirt

4. What's he wearing?   tie

5. What are they wearing?   raincoats

6. What's she wearing?   dress

7. What's he wearing?   jacket

8. What's she wearing with her
   sweater?   slacks

9. What are they wearing?   overcoats

Lesson 7

1. Reading and Oral Practice

A. Listen and repeat.

Does Ron like music?
Yes, he does. He likes music very much.

Does he like classical music?
Yes, he does. He likes classical music better than popular music.

Have there been any concerts at the college recently?
Yes, there have. There was a concert last night.

Did Ron go to the concert?
Yes, he did. He enjoyed it very much.

Did he go by himself?
No, he didn't. Sam went with him.

Are the concerts expensive?
No, they aren't. The students get a
special price.

Can Ron play a musical instrument?
Yes, he can. He knows how to play
the piano.

Does he play the piano well?
No, he doesn't. Music is just a hobby
for him.

Is he planning to become a musician?
No, he isn't. He's planning to become
a pharmacist.

B. Answer the questions.

1. Does Ron like music?

2. Does he like classical music?

3. Have there been any concerts at
the college recently?

4. Did Ron go to the concert?

5. Did he go by himself?

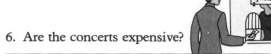

6. Are the concerts expensive?

7. Can Ron play a musical instrument?

8. Does he play the piano well?

9. Is he planning to become a musician?

C. Listen and repeat.

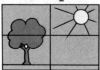

What color is the sky on a sunny day?
It's blue.

What color is the sky on a cloudy day?
It's gray.

What color is the sky at night?
It's black.

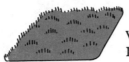

What color is grass?
It's green.

What color are carrots?
They're orange.

What color are tomatoes?
They're red.

What color are lemons?
They're yellow.

What color is snow?
It's white.

What color is chocolate?
It's brown.

D. Answer the questions.

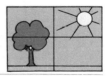

1. What color is the sky on a sunny day?

2. What color is the sky on a cloudy day?

3. What color is the sky at night?

4. What color is grass?

5. What color are carrots?

6. What color are tomatoes?

7. What color are lemons?

8. What color is snow?

9. What color is chocolate?

E. Dialogue.

NANCY: Did you go shopping at lunchtime?
CONNIE: Yes, I did. They had a sale on dresses at that little shop on Fifth Avenue.
NANCY: Did you find anything nice?
CONNIE: No, I didn't. I didn't really like their clothes too much.
NANCY: What's wrong with them?
CONNIE: Oh, the styles just don't suit me very well.
NANCY: Do they have a big selection?
CONNIE: No, they don't. That was one of the problems. They didn't have many dresses in my size.
NANCY: What size do you wear?
CONNIE: Size fourteen.
NANCY: Are their clothes expensive?
CONNIE: Yes, they are. There weren't any real bargains.
NANCY: Did you buy anything at all?
CONNIE: Well, yes, I did. I got a scarf.
NANCY: What color is it?
CONNIE: It's orange, brown, and yellow.

2. Structure and Pattern Practice

To answer *yes-no* questions in English, it is customary to use special short answer forms. Affirmative short answers consist of the word *yes* followed by the subject and the appropriate form of the auxiliary verb with which the question begins.

> *Is* he planning to become a pharmacist? Yes, he *is*.
> *Are* you going to the concert tonight? Yes, I *am*.
> *Did* he buy some records last week? Yes, he *did*.
> *Do* you like music? Yes, I *do*.
> *Can* you play the piano? Yes, I *can*.

Negative short answers consist of the word *no* followed by the subject and the negative contraction of the auxiliary used in the question.

> *Are* the concerts expensive? No, they *aren't*.
> *Have* you been to any concerts recently? No, I *haven't*.
> *Does* he want to be a musician? No, he *doesn't*.
> *Should* he stay home today? No, he *shouldn't*.

Note that contracted forms are NOT used in affirmative short answers, but that they ARE used in the negative. In the case of *I am*, the negative short answer is *No, I'm not*.

> Are you going to the movies tonight? No, I'm not.

Clothes is a plural noun.

> Her clothes are always very expensive.

Tomato is the singular form of *tomatoes*.

Exercises

A. Give affirmative short answers to these questions.

E X A M P L E
Is John a college student? *Yes, he is.*

1. Are you studying English today? (I)
2. Are they waiting for the bus?

3. Is it cloudy today?
4. Is there a calendar on your desk?
5. Were you absent yesterday? (I)
6. Were there a lot of bargains in the stores?
7. Does he like to play the piano?
8. Do you speak English in class? (we)
9. Did they attend the lecture?
10. Has he taken piano lessons?
11. Have you ever eaten at the college cafeteria? (I)
12. Had he seen his adviser before he paid his tuition?
13. Can you go to the concert with me? (I)
14. Should I send my cousin a birthday card? (you)
15. Will he get back on Saturday?
16. Was the sun shining this morning?

B. Give negative short answers to these questions.

E X A M P L E

Is John a computer programmer? *No, he isn't.*

1. Are you eating a sandwich? (I)
2. Is she taking care of the Wests' children tonight?
3. Are you studying Lesson Twelve today? (we)
4. Are there any students in the cafeteria now?
5. Was it sunny yesterday?
6. Was there a lot of work at the office last week?
7. Does Ann know how to play the piano?
8. Do you begin a new lesson every day? (we)
9. Did the bus stop at the corner?
10. Did you sleep late this morning? (I)
11. Has his car broken down again?
12. Have you known her for a long time? (I)
13. Had he looked at the schedule before he registered?
14. Can Ted fix the record player himself?
15. Should I miss the exam? (you)
16. Will he visit San Francisco on this trip?

3. Pronunciation and Intonation Practice

A. Listen and repeat.
**Contracted forms are used in affirmative statements
in normal conversation. When the speaker wants to**   61

emphasize the truth of a statement, or to contradict a negative statement, however, the full form is used and the stress is placed on the AUXILIARY.

E X A M P L E

(Teacher)   He is planning to be a musician.

(Students)   He is planning to be a musician.

(Teacher)   He is planning to be a musician.

1. I am writing my term paper.
2. He has taken piano lessons.
3. We have copied those sentences.
4. She had talked to her adviser.
5. I was listening to the teacher.

B. Repeat several times.

[ə] as the *u* in *bus*	[u] as the *oo* in *school*
hut	hoot
but	boot
mud	mood
skull	school
luck	Luke
sun	soon
ton	tune
rum	room

4. General Practice

Answer the questions about yourself and the people in your class.

1. What color is his shirt?
2. What color is his jacket?
3. What color is his sweater?
4. What color is her blouse?
5. What color is her skirt?
6. What color is her dress?
7. What color is her scarf?
8. What color is your pencil?
9. What color is your book?
10. What color is the wall?

Lesson 8

1. Reading and Oral Practice

A. Listen and repeat.

What was the matter with Mike last
  week?
He had a bad cold.

Was he really sick?
Yes, he was. He had a headache and
  a low fever.

What did the doctor tell him?
The doctor told him that he ought to
  stay in bed and sleep.

What did he tell Mike to drink?
He told him to drink a lot of water
  and orange juice.

What did he tell him to take?
He told him to take two aspirins every
  four hours.

What else did he say?
He said that Mike would be all right
 in a couple of days.

What did Mike try to do?
He tried to stay up and study for his
 exam.

What happened?
He couldn't keep his mind on the
 book.

What did he finally do?
He took the doctor's advice and went
 to sleep.

B. Answer the questions.

1. What was the matter with Mike
   last week?

2. Was he really sick?

3. What did the doctor tell him?

4. What did he tell Mike to drink?

5. What did he tell him to take?

6. What else did he say?

7. What did Mike try to do?

8. What happened?

9. What did he finally do?

C. Listen and repeat.

Where's the department store?
It's a little way down the street.

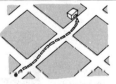

How far is it?
It's two blocks away.

Where's the bookstore?
It's around the corner on the right
side of the street.

Where's the drugstore?
It's on the next block on the left side of the street.

Where's the theater?
It's straight ahead.

D. Answer the questions.

1. Where's the department store?

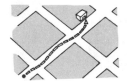

2. How far is it?

3. Where's the bookstore?

4. Where's the drugstore?

5. Where's the theater?

E. Dialogue.

JIM:	Where were you yesterday?
MIKE:	I was at home asleep.
JIM:	Asleep! I thought that you had to take an exam.
MIKE:	I was sick. I had a fever. I couldn't get out of bed.
JIM:	You still look a little sick. You ought to go back to bed.
MIKE:	I'm going now. I just came here to speak to my professor.
JIM:	What did he tell you?
MIKE:	He said that I'd be able to take a make-up exam.
JIM:	Well, that's all right then. Are you going straight home?
MIKE:	I have to stop at the drugstore on the way. I need some more aspirin.
JIM:	Do you think that you should walk that far?
MIKE:	I have to walk. I didn't bring my car. I didn't think I'd be able to drive today.
JIM:	Well, take care of yourself.
MIKE:	Okay. Thanks.

2. Structure and Pattern Practice

The verb phrase *to have to* is frequently used in place of *must*.

> She must register this week.
> She has to register this week.

Must has a present or future significance, whereas *have to* can be used in all tenses. Note that the question and negative forms are the same as those for *to have* when it is not followed by *to*.

> He has to study hard for the exam.
> Will we have to stay late tonight?
> She had to see her adviser last week.
> She didn't have to go shopping last week.

The negative form of *to have to* has a different meaning from the negative form of *must*.

> You mustn't talk here! (They don't permit you to talk here.)

> If you're sick, you don't have to take the exam. (It's not necessary to take the exam.)

Ought to is a frequent substitute for *should*.

> You should learn the new words.
> You ought to learn the new words.

The negative is *ought not to*.

> You ought not to drive today.

Be able to is a frequent substitute for *can*.

> You can get up tomorrow.
> You'll be able to get up tomorrow.

Could is the past tense form of *can*.

> I can't see you tomorrow.
> I couldn't see you yesterday.

Would is the past tense form of *will*.

> He says that he'll go straight home.
> He said that he'd go straight home.

Note that the contracted forms with *would* are the same as with *had* —*I'd, she'd, he'd,* etc. The negative contractions *wouldn't* and *couldn't* are generally used in conversation and informal writing.

To say and *to tell* have the same meaning, but differ in the structural patterns in which they are used. *To tell* is usually followed by an indirect object.

> What did he tell you to do?
> He told me to stay in bed.
> He told John that I'd been sick.

To say is not usually followed by an indirect object.

> She smiled and said hello.
> He said that he'd missed the exam.

When the person who was spoken to is identified after *to say*, the preposition *to* must be used.

> He said goodbye to me.
> What did she say to you?

The difference can be summed up in the statement that we tell someone something, but we say something to someone.

Irregular verbs introduced in this lesson are:

to drink	drank	drunk
to tell	told	told

Exercises

A. Change *must* to *have to* in these sentences.

EXAMPLE

She must see her adviser this week. *She has to see her adviser this week.*

---

1. I must go to New York on Thursday.
2. He must take an aspirin every four hours.
3. I must stop at the drugstore.
4. We must learn these new words.

B. Change to the past tense. Change the time expression to *yesterday*.

She has to see her adviser this week. *She had to see her adviser yesterday.*

1. We have to write a term paper next week.
2. He has to work late tonight.
3. They have to attend a meeting tomorrow.
4. I have to send him a postcard next week.
5. She has to write a lot of business letters today.
6. He has to take the car to the garage tomorrow.

C. Change *should* to *ought to*. If the original sentence is negative, make the new sentence negative.

They should study the new sentences. *They ought to study the new sentences.*

1. You should try to fix the record player yourself.
2. He should see a doctor right away.
3. You should drink a lot of orange juice.
4. He shouldn't get out of bed today.

D. Change *can* to *be able to*. Use the future with *will* in the new sentences.

He can get up tomorrow. *He'll be able to get up tomorrow.*

1. We can finish this lesson by Friday.
2. She can see her adviser next week.
3. You can borrow a typewriter from one of your friends.
4. You can write the letter in a few minutes.
5. I can buy some new clothes in January.
6. We can stay home on Sunday.

E. Change to the past.

He says that he'll visit San Francisco in October. *He said that he'd visit San Francisco in October.*

1. He says that he won't forget about the meeting.
2. He says that he can't sleep on airplanes.
3. His adviser says that she won't approve his schedule.
4. He says that we'll have a holiday on Monday.
5. The weather report says that it will rain tomorrow.
6. She says that she can make some money during the summer.
7. My adviser says that I can't major in physics.
8. She says that she can teach chemistry too.

F. Complete these sentences with the past tense form of *to say* **or** *to tell.*

E X A M P L E

He _____*said*_____ that he'd had a date with Ann.

1. She _____ that she wanted to make sure that the children were all right.
2. He _____ me that she'd laughed at all his jokes.
3. He _____ that they'd had a very good time.
4. The boss _____ goodbye to me before he left for Chicago.
5. He _____ me that he hadn't gone to San Francisco.
6. She _____ something to me, but I couldn't hear her.

3. Pronunciation and Intonation Practice

A. Listen and repeat.
In the present and past tenses, the auxiliaries *do, does,*
or *did* **are introduced into affirmative sentences and**
stressed when the speaker wishes to emphasize the
truth of a statement or to contradict a negative
statement.

E X A M P L E

(Teacher)   She does study every night.

(Students) She does study every night.

(Teacher)   She does study every night.

1. The sun did shine for a little while yesterday.
2. He does travel a lot.
3. I do try to solve the math problems.

4. She does laugh a lot.
5. They do take care of themselves.

B. Repeat several times.

[u] as the *oo* in *school*	[ʊ] as the *u* in *put*
fool	full
pool	pull
Luke	look
who'd	hood
stewed	stood
shoed	should

4. General Practice

Complete each question with a place in your city—a building, theater, or post office, for example—and answer the questions giving real information.

E X A M P L E

1. Is the _(theater)_ straight ahead or around the corner? (*It's around the corner.*)

2. Is the _____ on the right or the left side of the street?
3. Is the _____ three or four blocks away?
4. Is the _____ near the school or a long way from the school?
5. How far is it from the school to the _____?
6. Is the _____ near your house or a long way from it?
7. How far is it from your house to the _____?

Lesson 9

1. Reading and Oral Practice

A. Listen and repeat.

What's Steven West looking for?
He's looking for a report that he
    received last week.

Who did the report come from?
It came from a salesman who had just
    visited the Houston office.

Where did Jenny Black think that
    she'd put the report?
She thought that she'd put it in the
    files.

Where did Steve think that he'd left
    the report?
He thought that he'd left it on his
    desk.

How important is the report that
    they're looking for?
The report that they're looking for is
    very important.

Why does Steve want it?
He wants to check the sales figures which the salesman included in the report.

How accurate is the salesman who wrote the report?
The salesman who wrote the report is always very accurate.

Where has Jenny looked?
She's looked in all the files.

Where has Steve looked?
He's looked through all the papers that he keeps in his office.

What does he finally remember?
He finally remembers that he took the report home.

B. Answer the questions.

1. What's Steven West looking for?

2. Who did the report come from?

3. Where did Jenny Black think that she'd put the report?

4. Where did Steve think that he'd left the report?

5. How important is the report that they're looking for?

6. Why does Steve want it?

7. How accurate is the salesman who wrote the report?

8. Where has Jenny looked?

9. Where has Steve looked?

10. What does he finally remember?

C. Listen and repeat.

What color is her hair?
It's black.

What's he wearing on his head?
He's wearing a hat.

Why is there a smile on her face?
There's a smile on her face because
she's happy.

Why doesn't he need glasses?
He doesn't need glasses because his
eyes are very good.

What does she have around her neck?
She has a scarf around her neck.

What's he wearing on his feet?
He's wearing shoes on his feet.

What does he have on his hands?
He has gloves on his hands.

What does she have on her finger?
She has a ring on her finger.

Why are his legs sore?
His legs are sore because he ran all
the way to school.

Why is he doing those exercises?
He wants to build up his arm muscles.

Why does she have a sweater over
    her shoulders?
She has a sweater over her
    shoulders because she's cold.
What else does she have on?
She has a dress on.

D. Answer the questions.

1. What color is her hair?

2. What's he wearing on his head?

3. Why is there a smile on her face?

4. Why doesn't he need glasses?

5. What does she have around her
    neck?

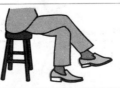

6. What's he wearing on his feet?

7. What does he have on his hands?

8. What does she have on her finger?

9. Why are his legs sore?

10. Why is he doing those exercises?

11. Why does she have a sweater over her shoulders?
What else does she have on?

E. Dialogue.

JOHN: Is this the report that you were looking for?
JENNY: No, that's not it.
JOHN: Have you found it yet?
JENNY: Yes, Steve remembered that he'd taken it home.
JOHN: How did he happen to do that?
JENNY: He put it in the briefcase that he always carries with him.
JOHN: At least it made us clean out the files.
JENNY: Did you come across a lot of old correspondence?
JOHN: Yes, we did. Some of the letters that we found were ten or fifteen years old.
JENNY: Well, I think that it's time to get rid of them.

2. Structure and Pattern Practice

Time clauses such as those introduced by *when, while, before,* and *after* are used as adverbs. Clauses that come after verbs like *say, tell, think,* and *remember* are the objects of those verbs. Clauses can also be used as adjectives. Adjective clauses are introduced by relative pronouns, and the three most frequently used relative pronouns are *who, which,* and *that.*

Who always refers to people.

> The salesman who wrote the report always sends in very accurate figures.
> I saw the girl who you'd told me about.

Which always refers to things.

> He looked through all the papers which he keeps in his office.
> He's looking for a report which he received last week.

That can refer either to things or to people.

> I saw the girl that you'd told me about.
> Some of the letters that we found were ten years old.

When *that* refers to people, it is usually the object of the verb (or a preposition) in the clause.

Note that an adjective clause follows the noun that it modifies.

To have on has the same meaning as *to wear,* but it is not used in continuous verb phrases.

> She has a scarf on.
> She's wearing a scarf.

Irregular verbs introduced in this lesson are:

to build	built	built
to run	ran	run

Exercises

A. Complete these sentences with *who* or *which.*

E X A M P L E

I don't know the student _____*who*_____ just went into the adviser's office.

1. He has a briefcase _____ he always carries with him.
2. The lesson _____ we just finished was an easy one.
3. The students copied the sentences _____ the teacher wrote on the blackboard.
4. The girls _____ were looking through the files couldn't find the report.
5. He'd taken home the report _____ we were looking for.
6. He's the policeman _____ directs traffic on this corner.

B. Change *who* or *which* to *that* in these sentences.

E X A M P L E

We got rid of all the correspondence which was more than ten years old. *We got rid of all the correspondence that was more than ten years old.*

1. I liked the girl who I saw in your office.
2. The exercises which he's doing will build up his muscles.
3. She has on the scarf which I gave her for her birthday.
4. My adviser is the professor who I had for chemistry last year.

C. Combine these sentences, using *who* or *which* to connect them. The second sentence should become an adjective clause.

E X A M P L E

He can't find the report. He received it last week. *He can't find the report which he received last week.*

1. They haven't received the office supplies. He ordered them last week.
2. I've never met the girl. She has on the yellow sweater.
3. The boys are late for school. They are running down the street.
4. He couldn't solve the problems. The math teacher had assigned them for homework.
5. I called the girl. She was taking care of the children.
6. The typewriter broke down. I borrowed it from Ted.

D. Combine these sentences, using *that* to connect them. The second sentence should become an adjective clause.

E X A M P L E

I haven't seen the letters. The boss wrote them yesterday. *I haven't seen the letters that the boss wrote yesterday.*

1. He smashed up the car. He'd borrowed it from a friend.
2. The doctor told him to stay in bed. He saw him yesterday afternoon.
3. The children are very young. She takes care of them.
4. The food wasn't hot. He got it at the cafeteria.
5. The professor is very popular with the students. Ted and John are talking to him now.
6. The homework was very difficult. The teacher assigned it last night.

3. Pronunciation and Intonation Practice

A. Listen and repeat.
When *not* is emphasized, the contracted forms are not usually used.

E X A M P L E

(Teacher)   I could not find the report.

(Students)   I could not find the report.

(Teacher)   I could not find the report.

---

1. We were not talking in class.
2. I have not seen that letter.
3. I cannot solve these problems.
4. He will not buy another used car.
5. He did not stay in bed.

B. Repeat several times.

[ə] as the *u* in *bus*	[ʊ] as the *u* in *put*
buck	book
luck	look
tuck	took
putt	put

4. General Practice

Answer the questions.

1. Is the lesson which we're studying now easy or difficult?
2. Was the lesson which we studied last week easy or difficult?
3. Is the book which you're using this year the same as the one which you used last year?
4. What color hair (eyes) does the person who's sitting next to you have?
5. Is the person who's sitting on your left taller or shorter than the person who's sitting on your right?
6. What color is the book that's on _____ desk?
7. What color is the pencil that's on _____ desk?
8. What color is the shirt that _____ has on?
9. What color is the dress that _____ has on?
10. What color is the skirt that _____ has on?
11. What color is the blouse that _____ has on?
12. What color is the sweater that _____ has on?
13. Are you taller or shorter than the student who's sitting next to you?
14. Are you younger or older than the student who's sitting next to you?

10
REVIEW

1. Review of Structure and Pattern Practice

A. Combine these sentences, using *when* to connect them. The first sentence should be changed to the past continuous.

E X A M P L E

I drove to school. I saw her on the corner. *I was driving to school when I saw her on the corner.*

1. I studied for the exam. I fell asleep.
2. They ran around the room. The teacher came in.
3. He read a book. The telephone rang.
4. He felt sick. He went home.

B. Combine these sentences, using *while* to connect them. Both sentences should be changed to the past continuous.

E X A M P L E

She smiled. I talked to her. *She was smiling while I was talking to her.*

1. I sat in the cafeteria. You attended the lecture.
2. He drove to work. He listened to the car radio.
3. She packed his bag. He dressed.
4. I slept. The teacher talked.

C. Give affirmative short answers to these questions.

E X A M P L E

Is the exam difficult? *Yes, it is.*

1. Have you looked at the sales figures? (I)
2. Are you waiting to see your adviser? (I)
3. Can you see the blackboard? (we)
4. Did they find the report?
5. Was there a lot of old correspondence in the files?
6. Were you listening to the radio in your car? (I)
7. Does he like classical music better than popular?
8. Had he read the report?

D. Give negative short answers to these questions.

E X A M P L E

Will he get back on Saturday? *No, he won't.*

1. Will those exercises build up his leg muscles?
2. Did she remember the new words?
3. Does he need glasses for his eyes?
4. Is she wearing slacks today?
5. Have you tried to fix the record player? (I)
6. Should they keep those old files?
7. Had he left the report on his desk?
8. Did he drink a lot of water?

E. Change *must* to *have to* in these sentences.

E X A M P L E

She must see her adviser this week. *She has to see her adviser this week.*

1. He must drink a lot of orange juice.
2. Must we wait in line?
3. They must clean out the files.
4. Must I put some air in the tires?

F. Change *should* to *ought to* in these sentences.

E X A M P L E

They should study the new sentences today. *They ought to study the new sentences today.*

1. You shouldn't park your car on the street.
2. He should take some work home from the office.
3. They should get rid of the old correspondence.
4. She shouldn't take a heavy schedule again next year.

G. Change *can* or *could* in these sentences to the appropriate form of *be able to*.

E X A M P L E

She couldn't find the report.   *She wasn't able to find the report.*

---

1. He can't solve those problems.
2. I can sleep late tomorrow.
3. He couldn't catch the early plane.
4. They couldn't find a good restaurant.

H. Change to the past.

E X A M P L E

He says that he'll stay in bed on Saturday.   *He said that he'd stay in bed on Saturday.*

---

1. She says that she can't find the report in the files.
2. He says that I won't be able to handle a heavy schedule.
3. They say they can't give me a new job yet.
4. He says that the salesmen won't have a meeting on Tuesday.
5. She says that she'll try to fix the record player herself.
6. He says that he can't order the supplies for a while.

I. Combine these sentences, using *who* or *which* to connect them. The second sentence should become an adjective clause.

E X A M P L E

He can't find the report. He received it last week.   *He can't find the report which he received last week.*

---

1. The students have to stand in line. They are waiting to pay their tuition.
2. The salesman is waiting to see you. He's sitting next to the door.
3. He didn't enjoy the concert. He attended it last night.
4. I've never seen the man. He's waiting to see the boss.
5. He doesn't like any of the cars. He's looked at them recently.
6. The job is much better than his old one. They've offered it to him.

J. Combine these sentences, using *that* to connect them. The second sentence should become an adjective clause.

I haven't seen the letters. The boss wrote them yesterday. *I haven't seen the letters that the boss wrote yesterday.*

1. I haven't met the girl. Ted and John are talking to her.
2. I want to see the report. You're looking at it.
3. He returned the book. He had borrowed it from Bill.
4. She put the furniture in the living room. She bought it at a special sale.
5. The women like to talk a lot. She goes shopping with them.
6. I have a present for the friends. I'm going to visit them this summer.

2. General Practice

Answer these questions with short answers.

1. Was it raining when you got up this morning?
2. Did you walk to school?
3. Did your English class begin at nine o'clock?
4. Is English your first class?
5. Have you finished studying Lesson Ten yet?
6. Do you have to study English every evening?
7. Will you have to take an English exam this year?
8. Can you speak English well?
9. Are you going to study other subjects next year?
10. Is English easy for you?

Lesson 11

1. Reading and Oral Practice

A. Listen and repeat.

Isn't this a new building?
Yes, it is.

Doesn't Dick work here?
Yes, he does. His company moved
  here last month.

Why didn't they stay in their old
  office?
It wasn't big enough.

Didn't Dick get a promotion recently?
Yes, he did. His boss transferred him
  to the accounting section.

Hasn't Dick studied computer
  programming?
Yes, he has. He studied programming
  at night school.

Did he study accounting too?
Yes, he had a course in accounting at
the same school.

Is he working as a programmer or an
accountant now?
He's working as a programmer.

Wasn't he a mail clerk before he got
his promotion?
Yes, he was. He didn't like that job
too well.

How does he like his new job?
He likes it very much.

Doesn't he live near the office?
No, he doesn't. He lives in another
section of the city.

How does he get to work?
Sometimes he drives and sometimes
he takes the bus.

Didn't he buy a new car recently?
No, he couldn't find one that he liked.

Won't he be able to buy one now that
he's had a promotion?
Yes, he'll probably start looking again.

B. Answer the questions.

1. Isn't this a new building?

2. Doesn't Dick work here?

3. Why didn't they stay in their old office?

4. Didn't Dick get a promotion recently?

5. Hasn't Dick studied computer programming?

6. Did he study accounting too?

7. Is he working as a programmer or an accountant now?

8. Wasn't he a mail clerk before he got his promotion?

9. How does he like his new job?

10. Doesn't he live near the office?

11. How does he get to work?

12. Didn't he buy a new car recently?

13. Won't he be able to buy one now that he's had a promotion?

C. Listen and repeat.

Where does she come from?
She comes from Mexico.
What's her nationality?
She's a Mexican.
Does she come from Mexico City?
No, she comes from Guadalajara.

Where does he come from?
He comes from Brazil.
What's his nationality?
He's a Brazilian.
Does he come from Rio de Janeiro?
No, he comes from Sao Paulo.

Where do they come from?
They come from Japan.
What's their nationality?
They're Japanese.
Do they come from Tokyo?
No, they come from Osaka.

D. Answer the questions.

1. Where does she come from?
   What's her nationality?
   Does she come from Mexico City?

2. Where does he come from?
   What's his nationality?
   Does he come from Rio de
   Janeiro?

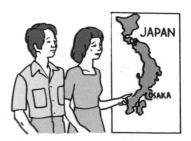

3. Where do they come from?
   What's their nationality?
   Do they come from Tokyo?

E. Dialogue.

JIM:	Isn't this the building where Dick works now?
SALLY:	Yes, it is.
JIM:	What time does he have lunch?
SALLY:	At about twelve, I think.
JIM:	Isn't it nearly twelve now?
SALLY:	It's a quarter to.
JIM:	Then why don't we have lunch with him?
SALLY:	He isn't expecting us. I didn't tell him that we were coming downtown.
JIM:	Why don't you call him now?
SALLY:	He probably has other plans. He's spent a lot of time looking for a new car lately.
JIM:	We can help him. I know a good place where they sell both new and used cars. It's only a few blocks away.
SALLY:	There's a telephone inside the building by the elevators. Why don't we call and tell him that we're here?
JIM:	All right, but let's have lunch before we start looking at cars. I'm hungry.

2. Structure and Pattern Practice

Negative questions are formed by placing the contracted form of the auxiliary verb and *not* at the beginning of the sentence.

> Hasn't he studied computer programming?
> Isn't he working in this building now?
> Can't he buy a new car now?

Don't and *doesn't* are used in the simple present tense and *didn't* in the simple past.

> Doesn't he like his new job?
> Don't you want to call him now?
> Didn't he get a promotion recently?

Why is a question word that is frequently used in negative questions.

> Why don't we wait and have lunch with him?
> Why can't he get a new car now that he's had a promotion?

To come from is an expression that is used to show origin, either a country or a specific area or city.

> She comes from Mexico.
> She comes from Guadalajara.

The nationality words—*American, English, Japanese, Brazilian, Mexican,* etc.—are always written with a capital letter in English, both when they are used as nouns or as adjectives.

> He's a Brazilian.
> We drink Brazilian coffee.

The following irregular verb is used in this lesson:

> to sell   sold   sold

Exercises

A. Change these affirmative yes-no questions to negative yes-no questions.

E X A M P L E

Have they moved to the new building? *Haven't they moved to the new building?*

1. Does he expect us for lunch?
2. Did the boss transfer him to the accounting section?
3. Has he studied accounting too?
4. Do they have lunch at noon?
5. Are they Japanese?
6. Can you call him now?
7. Does she come from Mexico City?
8. Should we wait for him by the elevators?

B. Change these negative statements to negative questions.

E X A M P L E

They didn't live in New York last year. *Didn't they live in New York last year?*

1. He hasn't found a new car that he likes.
2. He isn't wearing an overcoat today.
3. She isn't expecting to see us today.
4. There isn't a telephone near the elevators.
5. They don't have a cafeteria in the building.
6. They haven't sold their house.
7. I can't take an accounting course at night. (you)
8. She didn't get rid of the old correspondence.

C. Change these affirmative statements to negative questions.

E X A M P L E

They lived in New York last year. *Didn't they live in New York last year?*

works in a skyscraper downtown.
2. They come from Osaka.

3. He expected us to arrive at noon.
4. They sell both new and used cars here.
5. The salesman is writing a report.
6. She put the report in the files.
7. She can read the report in a few minutes.
8. He should leave the report on his desk.

3. Pronunciation and Intonation Practice

A. Listen and repeat.
Negative yes-no questions end with the same rising intonation pattern as affirmative yes-no questions.

E X A M P L E

(Teacher)   Don't they live in an apartment?

(Students)   Don't they live in an apartment?

(Teacher)   Don't they live in an apartment?

---

1. Didn't they move to a new office recently?
2. Hasn't he found a new car?
3. Can't we wait for him by the elevators?
4. Doesn't he come from Osaka?
5. Isn't he expecting us?

B. Repeat several times.

[b] as the *b* in *cab*	[p] as the *p* in *cap*
cab	cap
lab	lap
nab	nap
tab	tap
rib	rip
pub	pup
robe	rope

4. General Practice

Answer the questions.

1. What country does she come from?
   What city does she come from?
   Is she a Brazilian or a Mexican?

2. What country does he come from?
   What city does he come from?
   Is he a Brazilian or a Mexican?

3. What country do they come from?
   What city do they come from?
   Are they American or Japanese?

4. What country do they come from?
   What city do they come from?
   Are they American or Japanese?

5. What country do you come from?
   What city do you come from?

Lesson 12

1. Reading and Oral Practice

A. Listen and repeat.

Where's Laura West going?
She's going to the library.

She reads quite a lot, doesn't she?
Yes, she does. She reads two or three
    books a week.

Steve West enjoys reading too, doesn't
    he?
Yes, he does, but he doesn't have as
    much time for it as Laura does.

What does Laura like to read most?
She prefers fiction. She reads a lot of
    novels and short stories.

What about Steve?
He enjoys history, especially
    biographies of famous people.

Books from the library are free, aren't they?
Yes, anyone who lives in the city can get a library card.

The Wests don't buy many books, do they?
They buy a few. They belong to a book club.

How does a book club work?
The members can order books by mail.

What kind of books do they get from the club?
They get a lot of best sellers.

What's a best seller?
It's a book that's very popular for a time.

The books from the club are cheaper than the ones from a bookstore, aren't they?
Yes, a little.

Do the Wests buy any books from the bookstore in their neighborhood?
They buy paperback books there.

B. Answer the questions.

1. Where's Laura West going?

2. She reads quite a lot, doesn't she?

3. Steve West enjoys reading too, doesn't he?

4. What does Laura like to read most?

5. What about Steve?

6. Books from the library are free, aren't they?

7. The Wests don't buy many books, do they?

8. How does a book club work?

9. What kind of books do they get from the club?

10. What's a best seller?

11. The books from the club are cheaper than the ones from a bookstore, aren't they?

12. Do the Wests buy any books from the bookstore in their neighborhood?

C. Listen and repeat.

Where does she come from?
She comes from Venezuela.
What language do they speak in
  Venezuela?
They speak Spanish.

They speak Spanish in Colombia too,
  don't they?
Yes, they do. They speak Spanish in
  most of the countries of Central and
  South America.
But they don't speak Spanish in
  Brazil, do they?
No, they don't. They speak
  Portuguese in Brazil.

What do they speak in Canada?
They speak English and French in
  Canada.

There are people in the United States who speak two languages, aren't there?

Yes, there are a lot of people who speak both Spanish and English.

What about Japanese and Chinese?

A lot of people, especially in Hawaii and California, speak Japanese or Chinese as well as English.

D. Answer the questions.

1. Where does she come from?
   What language do they speak in Venezuela?

2. They speak Spanish in Colombia too, don't they?
   But they don't speak Spanish in Brazil, do they?

3. What do they speak in Canada?

4. There are people in the United States who speak two languages, aren't there?

5. What about Japanese and Chinese?

E. Dialogue.

LAURA: You haven't finished your coffee, have you?
STEVE: I'm still reading the newspaper.
LAURA: That's the financial section, isn't it?
STEVE: Yes, there's some interesting business news.
LAURA: But you've read the sports section, haven't you?
STEVE: Yes, I have. What are you doing?
LAURA: I'm going to throw away the sections we've read. The Sunday newspaper is so big!
STEVE: Well, save the entertainment section.
LAURA: What do you want it for?
STEVE: We may want to see the movie and TV programs for the week.
LAURA: Is there anything else you want?
STEVE: You didn't do the crossword puzzle, did you?
LAURA: No, I didn't. Do you want me to keep it?
STEVE: Yes, please. I may do it later.
LAURA: But let's go out for a walk now. It's a beautiful day.
STEVE: All right. It'll take me about fifteen minutes to get ready.

2. Structure and Pattern Practice

An attached question is a shortened question form which can be added to the end of any English statement. The auxiliary verb in the attached question corresponds to the one that would be used in the regular question form.

Affirmative statements are followed by negative attached questions.

> You got a new book in the mail today, didn't you?
> She's a member of a book club, isn't she?
> He reads the financial section every day, doesn't he?
> You've read this best seller, haven't you?

Negative statements are followed by affirmative attached questions.

> You don't take the subway to work, do you?
> He hasn't finished his coffee, has he?
> He won't be back before two, will he?
> There isn't any coffee, is there?

Negative attached questions are asked when an affirmative answer is expected, whereas affirmative attached questions are asked when a negative answer is expected.

> *Affirmative*   *Negative*   *Affirmative*
> They live in the city, don't they? Yes, they do.

> *Negative*   *Affirmative*   *Negative*
> They don't have a house, do they? No, they don't.

Note that the names of languages, like the nationality words, are always capitalized in English.

> They speak Portuguese in Brazil.
> That's a Spanish book, isn't it?

The following irregular verb is used in this lesson:

to throw (away)   threw   thrown

Exercises

A. Add the appropriate attached question to each of these affirmative statements.

E X A M P L E
They buy a lot of books, _don't they?_

---

1. There are a lot of stores in their neighborhood, _____
2. You've read this best seller, _____
3. She's a member of a book club, _____
4. He prefers reading history, _____
5. You can buy paperback books there, _____
6. She'll get ready in a few minutes, _____
7. He'll go to the post office this afternoon, _____
8. He bought some more books, _____

B. Add the appropriate attached question to each of these negative statements.

E X A M P L E
You didn't save the Sunday newspaper, _did you?_

---

1. You haven't thrown away the sports section, _____
2. She can't speak Spanish, _____
3. They don't belong to a book club, _____
4. He isn't expecting us, _____
5. There aren't any good TV programs this week, _____
6. He can't finish the crossword puzzle, _____
7. You don't have a library card, _____
8. She doesn't come from Venezuela, _____

C. Add the appropriate attached question to each of these statements. Then give the expected short answer.

E X A M P L E
They live in New York now, _don't they? Yes, they do._

---

1. You didn't see the boss today, _____ _____
2. He got a promotion recently, _____ _____

3. There was a lot of traffic this morning, _____ _____
4. You didn't tell him that we were coming downtown, _____
   _____

5. She enjoys reading, _____ _____
6. I can talk to the boss tomorrow, _____ _____
7. There isn't a telephone here, _____ _____
8. He can't speak Portuguese, _____ _____
9. She should throw away the old correspondence, _____
   _____

10. This biography isn't very interesting, _____ _____

3. Pronunciation and Intonation Practice

A. Listen and repeat: Attached questions can ask for confirmation of the statement that they follow, or they can ask for information. When they ask for confirmation, the rising-falling intonation of statements is used.

E X A M P L E

(Teacher)   They have a nice apartment, don't they?

(Students)   They have a nice apartment, don't they?

(Teacher)   They have a nice apartment, don't they?

1. She reads a lot, doesn't she?
2. You like fiction, don't you?
3. The book wasn't very interesting, was it?
4. You don't take the subway to work, do you?
5. She belongs to a book club, doesn't she?

B. Listen and repeat.
   When attached questions ask for information, the rising intonation of yes-no questions is used.

E X A M P L E

(Teacher)   You have a library card, don't you?

(Students)   You have a library card, don't you?

(Teacher)   You have a library card, don't you?

1. She hasn't thrown away that letter, has she?
2. That book is a best-seller, isn't it?
3. You read the newspaper every morning, don't you?
4. You haven't gone to the bookstore, have you?
5. Colombia is in South America, isn't it?

C. Repeat several times.

[n] as the *n* in *run*	[ŋ] as the *ng* in *thing*
thin	thing
win	wing
sun	sung
run	rung
ton	tongue
lawn	long

4. General Practice

Answer the questions.

1. Where does he come from?
   What language does he speak?

2. Where does she come from?
   What language does she speak?

3. Where do they come from?
   What language do they speak?

4. Where does he come from?
   What language does he speak?

5. What are the languages of Canada?

6. What is the language of the United States?
   What other languages do some people in the United States speak?

Lesson 13

1. Reading and Oral Practice

A. Listen and repeat.

Who did Dick have a date with last
    Sunday?
He had a date with Cathy.

What did they do?
They went sightseeing in New
    York City.

Where did they go?
They took a boat trip around
    Manhattan.

Is Manhattan an island?
Yes, it's surrounded by the Hudson,
    Harlem, and East rivers.

Are there many islands in New York?
Yes, most of the city is built on
    islands.

How do cars and trains get from one part of the city to another?
They go across bridges and through tunnels.

Is New York a seaport?
Yes, it's a very important seaport.

Did Dick and Cathy see any ships?
They saw a lot of them. The port of New York is used by ships from all over the world.

What else did they see?
They saw the skyscrapers in the financial district.

How long did the trip take?
It took four hours.

Did Dick and Cathy enjoy it?
Yes, they had a very good time.

Why did they like it?
They got a better view of the city than they had ever had before.

B. Answer the questions.

1. Who did Dick have a date with last Sunday?

2. What did they do?

3. Where did they go?

4. Is Manhattan an island?

5. Are there many islands in New York?

6. How do cars and trains get from one part of the city to another?

7. Is New York a seaport?

8. Did Dick and Cathy see any ships?

9. What else did they see?

10. How long did the trip take?

11. Did Dick and Cathy enjoy it?

12. Why did they like it?

C. Listen and repeat.

What's his shirt made of?
It's made of cotton.

What's his sweater made of?
It's made of wool.

What's her dress made of?
It's made of silk.

What's the table made of?
It's made of wood.

What are these new buildings made of?
They're made of steel, concrete, and glass.

What are telephones made of?
They're made of plastic.

What's their house made of?
It's made of brick and wood.

D. Answer the questions.

1. What's his shirt made of?

2. What's his sweater made of?

3. What's her dress made of?

4. What's the table made of?

5. What are these new buildings made of?

6. What are telephones made of?

7. What's their house made of?

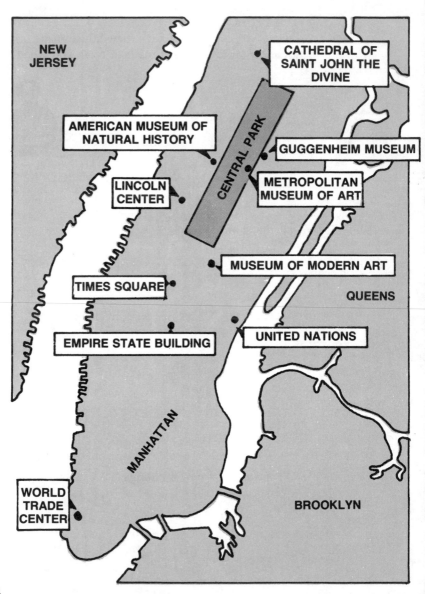

E. Dialogue.

ANA: Oh, there you are! I was looking for you all morning.
DICK: What's the matter?
ANA: Steve wanted you to attend a meeting, but you've missed it now.
DICK: When was it held?
ANA: It was finished an hour ago.
DICK: What was it about?
ANA: Some new accounting procedures were discussed.
DICK: I'm sorry I wasn't told about it yesterday.
ANA: Where have you been?
DICK: At the computer company.
ANA: What was going on there?
DICK: They're getting ready to put their new machines on the market.
ANA: Maybe you should explain that to Steve.
DICK: You're right. I'll go and talk to him right now.

2. Structure and Pattern Practice

The passive is generally used when the agent is either unknown, obvious to everyone, or not important to the meaning of the sentence. It is essentially an impersonal structure.

> The packages were delivered early.
> Her coat is made of wool.

When it is necessary to identify the agent, a prepositional phrase with *by* is used.

> The packages were delivered by the new mailman.
> Her dress was made by her mother.

The passive voice is formed with the auxiliary verb *to be* followed by the past participle. The present and past tenses of the passive are:

I am excused	we are excused
you are excused	you are excused
he is excused	
she is excused	they are excused
it is excused	

I was excused	we were excused
you were excused	you were excused
he was excused	
she was excused	they were excused
it was excused	

Questions in the passive voice are formed in the usual way, that is, by placing the auxiliary verb before the subject.

> Was the meeting held this morning?
> When was the meeting held?

Negatives in the passive are also formed in the usual way, by placing *not* after the auxiliary verb.

> I'm not excused from the meeting.
> He wasn't told about the meeting.

The following irregular verb is used in this lesson:

to hold   held   held

Exercises

A. Change these sentences to the passive. Do not change the tense. Do not use a prepositional phrase to express the agent if the subject of the original sentence is a pronoun.

E X A M P L E

They make clothes in New York.   *Clothes are made in New York.*

---

1. The boss wrote that letter.
2. The math teacher assigned the homework.
3. All the salesmen attended the meeting.
4. They deliver the mail at nine o'clock.
5. They open the store at half past nine.
6. Many people visit New York every year.
7. They built the city on an island.
8. His secretary checks all the letters.
9. Columbus discovered America.
10. They assigned me to a job in a bank in the financial district.

B. Change these sentences to the active. If no agent is expressed in the original sentence, use *they* as the subject.

E X A M P L E

The supplies are kept in a small office.   *They keep the supplies in a small office.*

---

1. New accounting procedures were discussed at the meeting.
2. The meetings are held in the boss's office.
3. The car was driven by his wife.
4. All the work was finished before three o'clock.
5. His letters are opened by his secretary before he sees them.
6. The report was read by everybody in the office.
7. The car was washed last week.
8. My book was borrowed by Mike.
9. The assignment was changed by the professor.
10. English is spoken in class.   117

C. Change these sentences to questions.

An island is surrounded by water. *Is an island surrounded by water?*

1. Most of the city was built on islands.
2. Their house is surrounded by stores.
3. The old correspondence was thrown away.
4. The packages were sent yesterday.
5. Several languages are spoken in the United States.

D. Change these sentences to the negative.

He was hurt in the accident. *He wasn't hurt in the accident.*

1. The sentences were written on the blackboard.
2. The students were excused by the professor.
3. The mail is delivered early in the morning.
4. Distance is measured in kilometers in the United States.
5. My typewriter was cleaned last month.

3. Pronunciation and Intonation Practice

A. Listen and repeat.
When two items following a verb are connected by *and*, *but*, or *or*, the first item normally is said with a rising intonation, and the second item is said with a rising-falling intonation.

(Teacher)   He bought a shirt and a coat.

(Students)   He bought a shirt and a coat.

(Teacher)   He bought a shirt and a coat.

1. I like math and science.
2. He has a new shirt and a new sweater.
3. I don't like math or history.
4. I can't find my pen or my pencil.
5. She bought apples but not oranges.

B. Repeat several times.

[ŋ] as the *ng* in *thing*   [ŋk] as the *nk* in *think*

ring	rink
rang	rank
sang	sank
sung	sunk
hung	hunk
sing	sink
sting	stink

4. General Practice

Answer the questions.

1. What's his sweater made of?   Wool

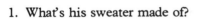

2. What's her blouse made of?   Cotton

3. What's the chair made of?   Wood

4. What are the skirts made of?   Wool

5. What's the wall made of?   Brick

6. What's the bridge made of?    Steel

7. What's her scarf made of?   Silk

8. What are the desks made of?    Steel

Lesson 14

1. Reading and Oral Practice

A. Listen and repeat.

Why is Dick so happy?
He's been promoted again.

Will he have more responsibility?
Yes, he's been given a lot more
  responsibility.

Why has he been promoted?
A new computer is going to be
  installed in the office.

Why do they want a new computer?
Computers are improved every year.

Is the new machine bigger than the
  old one?
It's bigger and better. A lot more work
  can be handled by the new
  machine.

121

Are they going to need more
programmers?
Yes, two more programmers have
been assigned to the section.

Who's going to be in charge of the
work?
Dick's going to be in charge of all the
programming.

When are they going to install the
new computer?
It will be installed next month.

Are any other machines going to be
used with the computer?
Yes, several other machines must be
installed to complete the system.

What else will be necessary?
A new air conditioning system will be
needed.

Why is that necessary?
The computer must be kept cool to
work properly.

Has any of the work been started yet?
Yes, they've started to put in the air
conditioning system.

When will all the work be finished?
It will all be finished in two months.

B. Answer the questions.

1. Why is Dick so happy?

2. Will he have more responsibility?

3. Why has he been promoted?

4. Why do they want a new computer?

5. Is the new machine bigger than the old one?

6. Are they going to need more programmers?

7. Who's going to be in charge of the work?

8. When are they going to install the new computer?

9. Are any other machines going to
   be used with the computer?

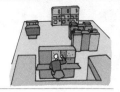

10. What else will be necessary?

11. Why is that necessary?

12. Has any of the work been started
    yet?

13. When will all the work be
    finished?

C. Listen and repeat.

What's this called?
It's called a pencil
What's it used for?
It's used to write with.

What's this called?
It's called a typewriter.
What's it used for?
It's used to write things so they can be
   read easily.

What are these called?
They're called telephones.
What are they used for?
They're used to talk across a distance.

What's this called?
It's called a computer.
What's it used for?
It's used to make mathematical
   calculations.
What else can it be used for?
It can also be used to solve other
   kinds of problems.
How can it be used in business?
It can be used to keep records and
   make out bills.

D. Answer the questions.

1. What's this called?
   What's it used for?

2. What's this called?
   What's it used for?

3. What are these called?
   What are they used for?

4. What's this called?
   What's it used for?
   What else can it be used for?
   How can it be used in business?

E. Dialogue.

TOM: Where have you been? You're almost an hour late.

DICK: I'm sorry. We had a lot of trouble at the office.

TOM: What happened?

DICK: I told you that they're installing a new air conditioning system, remember?

TOM: For your new computer? Yes, I remember.

DICK: Well, the old air conditioners were taken out this morning.

TOM: And the new ones weren't put in, right?

DICK: That's right. So it got hot in the office, and the computer broke down.

TOM: Were you able to fix it?

DICK: No. We're going to have to wait until tomorrow.

TOM: Is that when the new air conditioners will be installed?

DICK: Yes, first thing in the morning.

TOM: Well, let's go to the restaurant now. We won't be served after nine o'clock, and it's quarter to now.

DICK: Yes, let's hurry. I'm hungry.

2. Structure and Pattern Practice

In addition to the present and past, the passive can be used with other tenses, auxiliary verbs, and special verb phrases.

Present Perfect:	He has been assigned to the accounting section.
Past Perfect:	He had been promoted a year before.
Going to Future:	The computer is going to be installed on the twentieth floor.
Will:	All the work will be finished in two months.
Should:	The old correspondence should be thrown away.
Can:	Computers can be used to solve mathematical problems.
Must:	The report must be finished next week.
Have to:	The computer has to be kept cool to work properly.

In questions, the subject follows the FIRST auxiliary verb.

Has he been assigned to the accounting section?
Will the work be finished in two months?
Should the old correspondence be thrown away?

In the negative, *not* follows the first auxiliary verb.

The work on the computer hasn't been completed yet.
We won't be served at that restaurant after ten o'clock.

Exercises

A. Change these sentences to the passive. Do not change the tense. Do not use a prepositional phrase to express the agent if the subject of the original sentence is a pronoun.

E X A M P L E

They have installed a new computer. *A new computer has been installed.*

1. They have improved computers a great deal in the last few years.
2. They will install the other machines first.
3. They should complete the entire system next May.
4. An engineer should fix these machines.
5. They will give him a promotion next year.
6. They can give her more responsibility.
7. They will give a lot of accounting work to the computers.
8. They have to improve the system.
9. They're going to build a big new building here.
10. They ought to hold the meeting in a hotel.

B. Change these sentences to questions.

E X A M P L E

He has been assigned to the computer section. *Has he been assigned to the computer section?*

1. He will be given more responsibility.
2. Your record player can be fixed by the man at the store. (my)
3. These records can be handled by the new computer.
4. The inventory had been completed before they ordered the supplies.
5. The other machines in the system must be installed before the computer.
6. The class will be excused after an hour.

C. Change these sentences to the negative.

E X A M P L E

The old air conditioners have been taken out. *The old air conditioners haven't been taken out.*

1. He's been told about the meeting.
2. His car had to be fixed by the men at the garage.
3. This homework has to be finished today.
4. The mail has been delivered.
5. The assignment has been changed by the professor.
6. This correspondence can be thrown away.

3. Pronunciation and Intonation Practice

A. Listen and repeat.

When more than two items following a verb are given in a series, each item normally receives a rising intonation. The sentence-ending falling intonation does not occur until the last of the series.

E X A M P L E

(Teacher)   He bought a coat, some shirts, and a sweater.

(Students)   He bought a coat, some shirts, and a sweater.

(Teacher)   He bought a coat, some shirts, and a sweater.

---

1. She offered him coffee, milk, or water.
2. She went to the store to get bread, coffee, and milk.
3. They ordered paper, envelopes, and stamps.
4. I know a doctor, a lawyer, and an engineer.
5. I'm going to take physics, chemistry, or sociology next year.

B. Repeat several times.

[v] as the *v* in *leave*   [f] as the *f* in *leaf*

leave	leaf
five	fife
live	life
save	safe
have	half

4. General Practice

Answer the questions.

1. What's this called?
   What's it used for?

2. What's this called?
   Is it used to give the date or the time?

3. What's this called?
   Is it used to give the date or the time?

4. What's this called?
   Is it used to sit on or to eat on?
   What's it made of?

5. What's this called?
   Is it used to sit on or to eat on?
   What's it made of?

6. What's this called?
   Is it used for cars or office supplies?

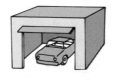

Lesson 15

REVIEW

1. Review of Structure and Pattern Practice

A. Change these affirmative yes-no questions to negative yes-no questions.

EXAMPLE

Have they finished their work yet? *Haven't they finished their work yet?*

1. Will he have a lot of responsibility in his new job?
2. Have computers been improved a lot?
3. Was the computer installed before the other machines?
4. Did they take a trip around Manhattan Island?
5. Have you seen the skyscrapers in the financial district?
6. Do they hold their meetings in the boss's office?

B. Change these negative statements to negative questions.

EXAMPLE

They didn't see many ships. *Didn't they see many ships?*

1. They don't have air conditioning in their office.
2. He hasn't bought a new coat.
3. He hasn't studied programming before.
4. I don't have enough time to read. (you)
5. She doesn't like to read fiction.
6. They can't buy all the new best sellers.

131

C. Change these affirmative statements to negative questions.

They moved to New York recently. *Didn't they move to New York recently?*

1. He's been put in charge of the computer section.
2. He spends all his time studying programming.
3. That book is a best seller.
4. I prefer to read biographies. (you)
5. The city is famous for its skyscrapers.
6. They had a good time.
7. He understands accounting procedures.
8. They've improved computers every year.

D. Add the appropriate attached question to each of these statements. Then give the expected short answer.

New York is a seaport, _isn't it?_ _Yes, it is._

1. He got a promotion last month, _____ _____
2. They haven't installed the computer yet, _____ _____
3. She always has a book with her, _____ _____
4. He hasn't fixed my typewriter yet, _____ _____
5. You belong to a book club, _____ _____
6. That book is about a famous woman, _____ _____
7. She hasn't thrown away the Sunday newspaper yet, _____ _____
8. She didn't finish the crossword puzzle, _____ _____
9. An island is surrounded by water, _____ _____
10. They've been assigned to the computer section, _____ _____
11. There's a bookstore in their neighborhood, _____ _____
12. He can't fix the machine, _____ _____
13. He won't be able to take the bus home, _____ _____
14. They won't be served after nine o'clock, _____ _____
15. She hasn't saved any money, _____ _____
16. They like to go sightseeing, _____ _____

E. Change these sentences to the passive. Do not change the tense. Do not use a prepositional phrase to express the agent if the subject of the original sentence is a pronoun.

E X A M P L E

They assigned him to the accounting section. *He was assigned to the accounting section.*

1. They've put him in charge of the office.
2. They're going to install air conditioning in the building.
3. They'll make copies of all the correspondence on these new machines.
4. His wife drove him to the airport.
5. They should finish the work in two months.
6. You can hear the concert on the radio.
7. They've returned all the books to the library.
8. They call this section of the city the financial district.
9. They use these machines to make copies of the correspondence.
10. Priestley discovered oxygen.

F. Change these sentences to the active. If no agent is expressed in the original sentence, use *they* as the subject.

E X A M P L E

The supplies are kept in a small office. *They keep the supplies in a small office.*

1. The repairs were made by a man in the office.
2. The homework was assigned by the chemistry professor.
3. All the accounting work is handled by computers.
4. The computer will be kept cool by the new air conditioning system.
5. Weight is measured in pounds in the United States.
6. She has been offered a better job.
7. The supplies will be ordered next week.
8. The packages should be delivered next week.
9. The letters had been thrown away by his secretary.
10. Books are sold in this store.

G. Change these sentences to questions.

E X A M P L E

Her dress is made of silk.   *Is her dress made of silk?*

---

1. The letter was sent to the wrong address.
2. They were given a lot of homework last week.
3. All the problems in the new system have been solved.
4. The new subway has been opened.
5. The computer will be used to keep records.
6. Islands are surrounded by water.

H. Change these sentences to the negative.

E X A M P L E

His shirt is made of wool.   *His shirt isn't made of wool.*

---

1. The lawyer has been paid for her work.
2. The package will be delivered today.
3. The meeting was held in Chicago.
4. He was told about the meeting yesterday.
5. Skirts and blouses had been put on sale.
6. The accounting will be handled by a computer.

2. General Practice

A. Answer the questions.

1. Where does she come from?
   What's her nationality?
   What language is spoken there?

---

2. Where does he come from?
   What's his nationality?
   What language is spoken there?

3. Where do they come from?
What's their nationality?
What language is spoken there?

B. Answer the questions.

1. What's this called?
Is it made of glass or concrete?

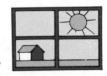

2. What's this called?
Is it made of wood or brick?

3. What's this called?
Is it made of wood or paper?
Is it used for sending or copying
letters?

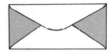

4. What's this called?
Is it made of glass or plastic?
Is it used for listening or watching?

INTERNATIONAL PHONETIC ALPHABET

CONSONANTS*

[p] — pie, hope, happy

[b] — bell, bite, globe

[f] — fine, office

[v] — vest, of, have

[k] — keep, can, book

[g] — go, get, egg

[l] — let, little, lay

[m] — man, must, dime

[n] — no, down, ton

[ŋ] — sing, ringing

[w] — water, we, one

[θ] — thin, three, path

[ð] — they, then, other

[s] — see, sat, city

[z] — zoo, does, is

[ʃ] — shoe, ship, action

[ʒ] — usual, garage

[tʃ] — change, watch

[dʒ] — June, edge

[r] — red, rich, write

[y] — you, yes, million

[h] — he, hat, who

[t] — ten, to, meet

[d] — do, did, sudden

VOWELS AND DIPTHONGS

[ɪ] — it, did, build

[i] — me, see, people

[ɛ] — end, let, any

[æ] — cat, bat, laugh

[ɑ] — army, father, hot

[ɔ] — all, caught, long

[ʊ] — book, full, took

[u] — too, move, fruit

[ə] — cup, soda, infant

[ɚ] — her, work, bird

[e] — say, they, mail

[o] — old, coal, sew

[ɑɪ] — dry, eye, buy

[ɔɪ] — toy, boy, soil

[ɑʊ] — cow, our, house

---

* [ə] and [ɚ] are used in this book for both stressed and unstressed syllables, [y] is used instead of IPA [j]. [ɑ] is used instead of IPA [a].

Vocabulary

The following list includes the words introduced in Textbook 3. The number indicates the page on which the word first appears.

able (to be able to), 67
accident, 15
accountant, 89
accurate, 74
across, 124
address (n), 31
advice, 64
agent, 15
air conditioner, 126
air conditioning, 122
almost, 4
American, 94
apartment, 31
arm, 77
asleep (to fall asleep), 43
aspirin, 63
(the) Atlantic (Ocean), 22
aunt, 20

bargain, 2
(to) be able to, 67
beautiful, 103

bed (to go to bed), 43
(to) belong (to), 99
best seller, 99
bill, 125
biography, 98
block, 65
blouse, 46
boat, 109
bookstore, 65
(to) borrow, 24
Brazilian, 91
(to) break (down) (broke, broken), 6
brick, 113
bridge, 110
briefcase, 79
(to) bring (brought, brought), 21
(to) build (built, built), 109
(to) build up, 77
(to) buy (bought, bought), 1

calculation, 125

California, 102
Canada, 23
card (birthday card), 20
carrot, 57
centigrade, 13
Central America, 101
(to) change, 14
(in) charge of, 122
cheap, 99
child (children), 43
chilly, 46
Chinese, 102
chocolate, 57
classical, 54
clothes, 59
club, 99
coast (n), 22
cold (n), 63
Colombia, 101
(to) come across, 79
(to) come from, 91
(to) compare, 4
compass, 21
(to) complete, 122

139

Appendix: Principal Parts of
Irregular Verbs

Simple Form (Present)	Past	Past Participle
to be (am, is, are)	was, were	been
to become	became	become
to begin	began	begun
to blow	blew	blown
to break	broke	broken
to bring	brought	brought
to build	built	built
to buy	bought	bought
to catch	caught	caught
to come	came	come
to cost	cost	cost
to cut	cut	cut
to do	did	done
to drink	drank	drunk
to drive	drove	driven
to eat	ate	eaten
to fall	fell	fallen
to feel	felt	felt
to find	found	found
to fly	flew	flown
to forget	forgot	forgotten
to freeze	froze	frozen
to get	got	gotten, got
to give	gave	given
to go	went	gone
to grow	grew	grown
to have	had	had
to hear	heard	heard
to hold	held	held

Simple Form (Present)	Past	Past Participle
to hurt	hurt	hurt
to keep	kept	kept
to know	knew	known
to leave	left	left
to lend	lent	lent
to make	made	made
to mean	meant	meant
to meet	met	met
to pay	paid	paid
to put	put	put
to read	read	read
to ride	rode	ridden
to ring	rang	rung
to run	ran	run
to say	said	said
to see	saw	seen
to send	sent	sent
to shine	shone	shone
to show	showed	shown
to sit	sat	sat
to sleep	slept	slept
to speak	spoke	spoken
to spend	spent	spent
to stand	stood	stood
to take	took	taken
to teach	taught	taught
to tell	told	told
to think	thought	thought
to understand	understood	understood
to wear	wore	worn
to write	wrote	written